Marie L Farrington

Facing the Sphinx

Marie L Farrington

Facing the Sphinx

ISBN/EAN: 9783337394707

Printed in Europe, USA, Canada, Australia, Japan

Cover: Foto ©Thomas Meinert / pixelio.de

More available books at **www.hansebooks.com**

FACING THE SPHINX.

BY

MARIE L. FARRINGTON.

"Ignorance and fear are the two hinges of all religion."—*Good Sense.*

PUBLISHED BY THE AUTHOR,
SAN FRANCISCO, CAL.,
1889.

TO MY BELOVED SON,
JOE W. FARRINGTON.
AFFECTIONATELY DEDICATED BY
HIS MOTHER.

DESCRIPTION OF THE FRONTISPIECE.

UNDER the foot of a youth lies a crocodile that symbolizes darkness, as opposed to light. It does not necessarily represent always the dark side of nature, but under this aspect the crocodile becomes the true ideograph of evil, for this is the source of spiritual blindness.

The youth who is portrayed as treading upon the crocodile, impersonates the newly-born sun. He was represented in an identical position by the Egyptians, who called him the "Young Horus," and from them the Gnostics derived their mythical Christ, the abstract principle which conveyed an idea of re-birth, of regeneration. This is an occult phraseology replete with arcane significance.

The Christ and the cross were both linked closely together, because these two words are synonymous. They found an outward expression in the visible sun, when in the act of crossing the ecliptic.

It is a generally well-known fact that our sun entered the sign of Pisces in the year 155 B. C., and that since that event occurred, the fish has been an emblem interwoven with the symbolism which is derived from the Christ. Therefore, the Catholic Church has especially preserved the emblematical fish as it existed before the establishment of Christianity.

The Egyptians, who were most proficient in astronomy and mathematics, represented Horus as the personified sun entering the sign of Pisces, in the act of rising in the heavens, hence dispelling darkness, as typified by the crocodile. The youthful sun was necessarily born in spring, at Easter. He carried upon his own head the image of the zodiacal division into which he had just entered, to tarry thither 2,155 years.

The three fingers uplifted indicate plainly that this image refers to the unification of the threefold sun, as impersonification of the trinity in unity. It was verified once a year, at the spring equinox, when the new-born Horus rose from the dead, on the horizon of the resurrection.

In the catacombs, an old Christ and a youthful one were discovered, which is a remarkable coincidence, proving to a certain extent that the early Christians recognized the threefold principle of the Christ type.

It is obviously useless to remind our readers that the abstract idea just enunciated has naught to do with the personality of Jesus Christ. If we refer frequently in this work to the ceremonies and emblems of the Romish Church, it is solely because they are remnants of the symbolism of ancient races. We neither uphold the theories bearing on the reality of Jesus' life on earth, nor wish to argue the veracity of the writings relating to his remarkable career. Our frontispiece is intended to convey both the exoteric and the esoteric imagery of the Christ idea, as conveyed by the wise men of bygone ages. It was bequeathed by them to posterity as an imperishable memento of their knowledge in the realms of occultism.

In the year 2000 A. D., the sun will leave Pisces to enter the sign of Aquarius, facing at the same time Leo. According to certain Kabalists, the world will then be ushered into an era of quiet strength and superior attainments.

INTRODUCTION.

DANTE, in his poem upon Paradise, relates that the Supreme Being appeared to him under the geometrical figure of three circles. The latter formed an iris, whose lively colors generated each other, but while he gazed steadily upon the dazzling light emanating from them, he could perceive nothing but his own shadow reflected by a well-understood process. Thus, while adoring God, man worships his own image, issuing from the kingdom of darkness, misnamed "Theology." Therefore, as long as the clouds of darkness, or ignorance, its equivalent, will hang over the human mind, so long will tarry the empire of Evil among us. Knowledge alone will dispel the thick mist shadowing the bright Sun of Wisdom.

The only aim of this book is to foster the study of symbolism, and of the inner interpretation of the so-called Sacred Scriptures. In the first excitement caused by the revelations made by the theosophical leaders, many of their adherents took a stand against the Bible, reviling it in the most profligate terms. Their indignant outburst sprung from their innocence from "eating of the book." We readily excuse them, for there are still many people who call themselves well educated, and yet will declare with the greatest ingenuity that "even a child can understand the Bible." This statement is so ludicrous that it becomes a rather difficult task to comment upon it, because those people are so rooted in their prejudices that they have built almost an insurmountable barrier between their narrow-minded world, and light and truth.

We have no greater teacher than the heavens and nature. These are the two great books which contain the wisdom of all nations. The key to them unravels the mysteries of all ages, and the sooner the world at large is convinced of the truth of our assertion, the better it will be for our present race. Therefore, we offer the present study of symbology to the public, not as a complete and exhaustive treatise of such a complex system of thought, but as a modest effort towards helping others still less favored than ourselves.

We have followed in the footsteps of learned scholars who have preceded us in the same useful field, and we present the result of their researches in the most comprehensible way allowed by such a deep subject.

If we contribute our mite towards the revival of the ancient mode of thought, which can be found partly in the Bible, if understood, and partly in the sacred and profane literature of Egypt, India, Persia, Chaldea, Central America, China, Greece, Rome, etc., we will be amply rewarded. For to dispel the clouds of ignorance which are still hanging over the human intellect, is to conquer and uproot wickedness. Let us eat of the fruit of the "tree of Paradise," so that, by acquiring the knowledge of good and evil, we may always be wise enough to choose good and eschew evil.

THE AUTHOR.

San Francisco, July 7, 1889.

CONTENTS.

DESCRIPTION OF THE FRONTISPIECE.

INTRODUCTION.

CHAPTER I. FACING THE SPHINX. The Masculine Sphinx was not the Primitive Type; Cosmogony and Anthropogenesis; Totem Signs; The Eternal Celestial Book; Astronomy *versus* Symbology; Keys to the Jewish Scriptures; The Concessions of the Romish Church; The Age of the Earth; The Age of Mankind; Darwin's Opinion; The Earth's Periods; Evolution; Gaudry's Opinion; Continental Glaciers; White and Black Types; Seventeen Pre-historical Men; A Monstrous Snake and a Gigantic Man; Palæolithic Arts; Neolithic Lake Dwellers; A Miocene Civilization; The Eocene Age. ....

CHAPTER II. CONTINENTS. The Zodiac of Denderah; The Sidereal Year; The Egyptians' Mastery of Exact Sciences; Central Americans and Egyptians Had a Common Origin; The Ancient Races of Central America; The Ballet of the Tapirs; The Importation of Tapirs to America; Symbolism of the Palm: Atlantis was a Continent; The Evolutionary Phases of the Earth; The Cyclic Law; A Cataclysm that Lasted 150,000 Years; The Birth of Africa; The Magnus Annus; Destruction by Water and by Fire; Biblical Theories; The Hyperborean Continent; Amber, The Stone of the Sun; The Origin of Numbers......

CHAPTER III. PAST, PRESENT, AND FUTURE RACES. What is Creation? The Mosaic God; Our Earth; Space; Quiché Manuscript; The Name of God; Universal Laws; The "Heart of Heaven;" The Central Sun; Plato's Anima Mundi; The Life Center; The Mexican Four Creations; The Three Quiché Creations; Causes and Effects; The Birth of Man; The Early Giants; The Missing Link; Separation of Sexes; The Nabathean Agriculture; The Disrespectful Son; Adam the

(ix)

Red; The Four Adams of Genesis; The Teachings of a Double Doctrine..................

CHAPTER IV. THE SACRED SCRIPTURES. Mythology *versus* Religion; Too Much Light is Hurtful to the Eyes; The Three Oldest Religions; The Youngest Revelation; Josephus' Pretensions; The Fable of Moses; The Central American Giants; Pagan Gods; The Greater and Lesser Mysteries; The Measure of Time a Secret; The Keys to the Sacred Scriptures; The Pentateuch; The Word Era; The Christian Era; The Essenes; How the New Testament was Gotten Up; The Double Sense System; Origin of the Sacraments.........

CHAPTER V. TYPOLOGY AND SYMBOLOGY. The Seven Keys of Symbolism; Madame Blavatsky's Definitions; Two Great Symbologists; The First Sense; Onomatopœia; Totemism; Religion's Origin in Awe; Evolution of Symbolism; What is God? The Circle; The Dance of the Tapirs; Votan's Circle; The Brahmanical Egg; The Circle and the Planets; Ezekiel's Wheel; The Masons' Mystic Chain; The Wedding Ring; The Decimal System; The Master Masons' Grip; The Ten Sephiroth; The Gnostics' Pleroma; The Pythagorean Decade; The Tetragrammaton....

CHAPTER VI. NUMBER 3 AND NUMBER 7. The Weather gods; The Seven Elements; Masterpieces of Occultism; The Value of Names; The Number Par Excellence; Ragon's Definitions of the Triangle; Trinosophists; Kabalistic Trinity; Mythical Trinity; Starry Triangle; Natural Trinity; The Two Universes; Three Mystic Letters; Taking an Oath; The Nimbus or Glory; The Papal Blessing; Solomon's Seal; Microprosopus; Seven Letters; Seven Astronomically; The Seventh Day; Fiat Lux; The Seven Stars of Ursa Major; Moses and Number Seven; The Pleiades and the Atlantides; The Golden Calf; Seven Principles; Seven Kings of Edom; Niobe and Latona; Apollo; Jehovah; The Music of the Spheres; Revelation....

CHAPTER VII. THE DRAGON, THE SERPENT, AND THE CROSS; The Woman of Revelation and Latona; Lemuria and Atlantis. The "War in Heaven;" The North Pole and the South Pole; Survival of the Mythical Dragon in China; The Serpent of the Ophites; The Great Bear and the Little Bear; A-Draconis; The Unicorn; The National Arms of England; The Seven-

Headed Dragon; The Beast of Revelation; Wisdom in Numbers; Three Letters S. S. S; Evolution in Symbology; The Virgin with Her Babe; Origin of the Easter Eggs; Renewal-Votan, the Serpent; The Hole of a Snake; The Great Sea; The Tree of Knowledge; Chnouphis; The Modern Bracelet; The Brazen Serpent; The Astral Light; Duality in Man..................

CHAPTER VIII. THE SQUARE, THE TREE, AND THE MOUNT. The Father as the Tetrad; the Mother with Her Child; The Gnostic Square; The Four Beasts of Revelation; Ezekiel's Vision; The Four Evangelists; the Squaring of the Circle; Jehovah, the God of the Four Letters; the Tonsure of the Priests; The Tree of Paradise; The Clothing of Man; The Fall; Prometheus; The Secrets of the Kabala; The Quiché Tree; The Dodecahedron; The Ark; The Tree as an Oracle; The Tree of the Prophets; The Gooseberry Bush; The Palm; Eating the Book; Drunkenness; Origin of the Christian Communion; The Mount; The Bad Woman of Hong Kong; Jacob's Pillar; The Phallus; Gabriel's Lily; The Christmas Tree......................................

CHAPTER IX. THE CROSS. The Tau and the Astronomical Cross; Our Christmas Trees; The Cross as Natural Symbol; Nilometer; Quartering of Arms; Biblical References to the Cross; The Four Corners of Revelation; An Initiation Ceremony Surviving in the Romish Church; The Southern Cross; The Lamb or Ram; The Fish, the Bull, and the Scorpion; The Balance or Scales and the Zodiak of Denderah; Two Catholic Festivals; Virgo; Two Christs; The Numerical Value of the Name Christ; The Sun and the Moon; Romish Blazonry; Creeping on all Fours; The Egg and the Cross; The Jews Borrowing from the Egyptians; The Svastica; The Masons' Gavel; The Stauros; The X; The Conversion of Constantine; The First Crucifix; The Gnostic Christ; The Initiation; The Immaculate Conception....................................

CHAPTER X. SYMBOLICAL NUMBERS CONTINUED, 5, 6, 8, 9, 12. The Pentagram and the Pentagon; The Five Limbs of a Man; Capricornius; Akasa; The Dual Priapus; Several Resurrection Myths; St. Paul's Symbolical Teachings; The Cherubims of Glory; The Hebrew Tabernacle; David's Dance; The Argha;

The Holy Virgin Mary; The Nave of the Church; The Lingha and Yoni; The Lotus, The Letter M; Aquarius; The Hexagon; The Six Powers of Nature; Six-headed Gods; Leo; The Woman Sitting upon a Scarlet-colored Beast; The Beast Loses One Head; The Third Beast; The Ogdoad; The Caduceus; Melchizadek; Hermes; Nine Splendid Lights; Paradise According to the "Book of God;" The Dodecahedron; The Twelve Signs of the Zodiac; The Twelve Wonders of Hercules; Twelve Manner of Fruits; Number 13..................

CHAPTER XI. ANCIENT AND MODERN PHILOSOPHICAL SCHOOLS. The Greek Philosophers and the Gnostics; Epicureans; Academics; Stoics; Aristotelians; Platonists and Eclectics; Alexandria; Codices Alexandrini; St. Paul's Denunciations; The Monogram I. H. S.; The Gnosis; Theosophy; Its Aim; Re-incarnation and the Law of Karma; The Original Sin; The Mysteries; Jesus Advocating the Doctrine of Re-incarnation; Sinnett's Opinion; Madame Blavatsky's Theory; Dr. Anna Kingsford's Ideas on the Same Subject; How Karma is Generated; The Atonement for Sin; The Eye of Providence; What Regulates the Events of One's Life; A Doctrine with Double Meaning.

CHAPTER I.
"FACING THE SPHINX."

"They needs must find it hard to take truth for authority who have so long mistaken authority for truth."

A GENERAL version of the myth of the sphinx, adopted by popular writers on Greek mythology, is the following: " The origin of the myth of the sphinx was not definitely known even to the ancients. The sphinx itself was probably a religious symbol of the Egyptians, which was transferred to Greece, and subsequently underwent a change of meaning. Among the Egyptians the sphinx seems to have been a symbol of royal dignity, betokening a combination of wisdom and strength; by the Greeks, however, it appears to have been regarded as a symbol of the burning, pestilence-breeding heat of the summer sun. The form, which was that of a lion, generally in a recumbent position, with the breast and upper part of a beautiful woman, was an imitation of the original male sphinxes of Egypt. Ancient Egyptian art reveled in the creation of colossal sphinxes, which were carved out of granite. A notable example of this kind exists in the giant sphinx near the Pyramids of Gizeh, which is eighty-nine feet long. Moreover Greek art was only acquainted with the sphinx in its female form, and departed from the Egyptian type by adding wings to the lion's body." This statement is utterly erroneous. We will prove subsequently that the Egyptian sphinx was at first feminine, a fact conclusively established by typology. It became masculine in a later stage of symbolism, when primeval conceptions, or rather truisms, were undergoing an evolutionary transformation, which did not affect the neighboring countries immediately. They had adopted the primitive emblem of the sphinx from the Egyptians, who thus embodied the greatest principle underlying their philosophical system. It is supremely ridiculous to fancy that a nation standing foremost as the center of a high civilization should have adopted meaningless symbols, for such would they have been, if their true significance could not have been fathomed.

Modern times have produced many Œdipuses who have endeavored to interpret the riddle of the sphinx, and the apparently incongruous theogonies of by-gone ages. The most popular authors, including Max Müller, who have expounded the mythologies of the ancients, have adhered to the unreasonable theory that every emblem had been invented by the diseased imagination of insane people, or must be explained either as a solar or a phallic glyph. But science progresses in giants' strides. Every age has produced at the transitory stage, men capable of opening a new path through the entangled vines of a forgotten road; those are thinkers who do not mistake authority for truth. Still their task is arduous; they have to fight century-old prejudices, for we are all endowed with an extremely finite intelligence, and it requires strenuous efforts on our part to grasp what stands outside of the range of our most approved educational methods. Furthermore, it becomes almost impossible to convey to certain people a glimpse of scientific facts when clashing with their own routine and worn-out theories.

Men well versed in mythological lore, such as Gerald Massey and Gaston Maspero, have proven, without the shadow of a doubt, the common origin of religions and languages. In the cosmogony and the anthropogenesis of mankind, we find irrefutable evidences that no religion was ever based on fiction, or was the sequence of a special revelation. Archæology has demonstrated that no Egyptian papyrus, Indian tolla, Assyrian tile, or Hebrew scroll should be accepted literally; that they are not a mere product of the fantastic imagination of anybody. Even nursery tales and superstitious reminiscences of ancient times have been traced back to their original source by typology, as surely as heraldry is conclusively shown as being derived from totem signs. "The thing that has been, it is that which shall be, and that which is done, is that which shall be done, and there is no new thing under the sun."—*Ecclesiastes, chap. 1.*

The ancients had a profound knowledge of natural and cosmic laws which they illustrated in their religious, or rather philosophical, systems. When we will understand them thoroughly, they will unravel to us the bulk of the primitive archaic wisdom. Of all the sciences which have contributed to the present impetus given to researches into the cosmogonies of antiquity, geology, astronomy, and archæologyst and foremost. "Why does not someone teach me the constellations, and make me at home in the starry heavens, which are always overhead, and which I do not half know to this day," says Carlyle. This just desire to be made conversant with a subject forever open to our observations, would naturally lead to a more thorough investigation. Stars, moons, suns divulge to us every day, and at every instant, the hidden secrets of the past, present, and future. They are the "eternal celestial book," the only true revealers of mysteries, which, if fathomed, would unravel the beginning of our universe. It is not sufficient to know the constellations, for their names have left such a strong impression upon the human mind that an inquiry into their history throws a flood of light on the most important problem of modern times. They are indissolubly linked with symbology. Not one of these three sciences, *i. e.*, astronomy, geology, and archæology, can be comprehended without the aid of the two others.

"One great incentive to the study of astronomy

will yet be to find out at first hand, what the Kamites typified in the book above with which we have been so deluded at second hand below," says the great lecturer, G. Massey. Verily no greater truth was ever uttered. Some day, not very far off, leaders in educational circles will perceive the absolute necessity of explaining astronomy by a compendium on symbolism and typology. Then a deviation from the old routine will produce startling results. History will be forced to alter its chronology, or rather correct its ridiculous anachronisms. The old tottering edifice built upon errors, that were bequeathed to us by centuries of gross ignorance, will tumble never to rise again. In the intellectual struggle which is ever progressing towards higher attainments and greater discoveries, the worst stumbling-block has been theological intolerance. The masses have been educated into accepting as truth, what was propounded to them with authority. But a few years ago the Bible was considered infallible on all matters pertaining exclusively to science. Educated persons undoubtedly do not believe any more in the literal sense of the creation of the world in six days, but they have not advanced very far from their starting-point. Now that geology, astronomy, archæology, and ethnology present cumulative evidences that upset entirely the accepted doctrines, why do theologians fight truth so stubbornly? Keys to the Jewish Scriptures have been re-discovered, and it is only a question of a few years when the most ignorant ones will be able to read the Bible in its true meaning. The Catholic Church, foreseeing wisely the results of too abrupt a transition, has already come out with a declaration which is intended to smooth the way to concessions. The learned Abbé Favre, in one of his eloquent lectures delivered at the Sorbonne, has categorically declared that "palæontology and archæology may, without detriment to the veracity of the Holy Scriptures, discover traces of pre-adamic man in the tertiary beds. Since the Bible disregards all creatures anterior to the last deluge but one, we are left free to admit the existence of man in the grey diluvium, in Pliocene, and even Eocene strata." It is surely an easy way of preparing an honorable surrender to the well-established fact of the antiquity of man on this earth.

If we consider that, according to Biblical reckonings, the deluge took place 2,448 years B. C., and the world's creation 4,004 years B. C., and that the most accurate researches of geologists and physicists have led them to assign to our globe an existence of at least 10,000,000 years (Sir W. Thomson), we will have sufficient ground to wonder at such disproportionate data. Moreover, one of our most learned geologists, Mr. Huxley, considers the minimum adopted by Sir W. Thomson as unsatisfactory. He expresses his own opinion that, according to the laws of evolution, no less than 1,000,000,-

000 of our solar years have elapsed since vegetation appeared on our little planet.

Mr. Darwin, in his "Descent of Man," says, " . . . an ape nearly as large as a man, namely, the Dryopithecus of Lartet, which was closely allied to the anthropomorphous Hylobates, existed in Europe during the Upper Miocene period; and since so remote a period the earth has certainly undergone many great revolutions; and there has been ample time for migrations on the largest scale.

"At the period and place, whenever and wherever it may have been, when man first lost his hairy covering, he probably inhabited a hot country; and this would have been favorable for a frugivorous diet, on which, judging from analogy, he subsisted. We are far from knowing how long ago it was when man first diverged from the catarrhine stock, but this may have occurred at an epoch remote as the Eocene period; for the higher apes had diverged from the lower apes as early as the Upper Miocene period, as shown by the existence of the Dryopithecus." Mr. Darwin's opinion being thoroughly indorsed by many scientific men of high standing, the passage just quoted justifies anthropologists for assigning to man a hoary ancestry.

Though frequently mentioned in standard works, the exact duration of the different periods of the earth's formation is not established, even approximately. For those unacquainted with the geological divisions of the epochs corresponding to our planet's evolutionary phases, we will give them as follows:—

Primordial { Laurentian, Cambrian, Silurian.

Primary { Devonian, Coal, Permian.

Secondary { Triassic, Jurassic, Cretaceous-chalk.

Tertiary { Eocene, Miocene, Pliocene.

Quaternary { Palæolithic man, Neolithic man, Historical period.

Evolutionary laws as expounded by Darwinists, are not accepted by all scientists as an absolute truth; it is simply a hypothesis held by Paracelsus, and before him by many sages of antiquity, which rests on a solid basis, if we except the ape theory. Natural selection has not been sustained either; it has been upset considerably by prominent scientific men, among whom stand foremost M. de Quatrefages and Danilevsky. Anthropologists are at variance also concerning the age of man, their estimates varying from five hundred thousand down to fifty thousand years. This divergence of opinions, however, affects only details, the main result is illustrated daily in the disappearance of ignorance and the production of new evidences tending to rectify mistakes and harmonize scientific theories.

Gaudry, in his book "Modern Science," says that the oldest skulls and skeletons which date from the glacial period, are probably at least one hundred thousand years old. They are specimens of a fine race, tall in stature, large in brain, and on the whole superior to many existing races of mankind; thus disproving our descent from the ape, but not the fundamental laws of evolution.

Professor Winchell's opinion as to the antiquity of the Mediterranean race is also worthy of more than a passing remark. He believes that the white race made its appearance during the later decline of the continental glaciers; but he adds, at the same time, that "this does not concern the antiquity of the black and brown races, since there are numerous evidences of their existence in more southern regions, in times remotely pre-glacial." "Yet we have abundant proofs that the black race overran Europe at an unknown epoch, for the types of skulls found there have been of two kinds: the ortho-gnathous and the prognathous, or the Caucasian and negro types. This authenticated fact is greatly in favor of Darwin and Gerald Massey, the great symbologist; both hold that every custom, symbol, and religion can be traced back to Inner Africa; the latter gentleman endorsing consequently the famous saying of Rev. Robert Taylor: "Bind it about thy neck, write it upon the tablet of thy heart, everything of Christianity is of Egyptian origin."

By forcing mother earth to lay bare her bosom, priceless treasures have been brought out of the excavations, as in the department of the Haute-Garonne, where a wonderful scene of by-gone ages was brought to light. Squatting near the remains of a coal fire, seventeen men were discovered in company with antediluvian mammals. They wore amulets around their necks, and the broken pottery scattered around the place testified to their knowledge of certain arts common to civilized races.

Though the word palæolithic means earlier stone-age, the name itself is an anomaly. Extant relics of that epoch are, it is certain, very scarce thus far; but they are decidedly artistic. In the Thayngin grotto, Switzerland, an excellent sketch of a reindeer feeding has been unearthed. It is at least five hundred thousand years old, and it would do credit to any modern animal painter. The engraving of the head of a horse, also, reveals talent. With the surprises the future reserves to explorers, the artistic skill displayed in the relics which have been recovered from the cave-dwellers, may induce scientists to reconsider their preconceived idea concerning the civilization of the Palæolithic races.

But a short time ago a very important discovery

was made by a French citizen residing in Gainesville, Texas. Having occasion to sink a well, he selected a spot in a valley near a ravine of great length. During heavy rains it is transformed into a raging torrent which deposits in the valley limestone, gravel, mud, and all sorts of *débris*. After reaching a depth of four feet in a limestone formation, Mr. Sommes (such was the name of the French gentlemen) came upon the vertebræ and ribs of an animal of the size of a small pig's ribs, only it was of a tapering shape. Monsieur Sommes proceeded carefully in the work of unearthing the bones toward the tapering end, and successfully uncovered seventeen rattles, the largest one measuring six inches across. Then people congregated at the place; brought thither by the strange discovery, they eagerly helped in the work of unearthing the remains of the monster. After uncovering nineteen feet, judge of their surprise when they perceived the skeleton of a gigantic man in the stomach of the huge reptile. The remains of both are well preserved, as perfect, in fact, as when first denuded of flesh. Near the bones of the man's right hand is a stone hatchet very similar to those found among the implements pertaining to Palæolithic races. Let those who believe in a first man, called Adam, ponder over this unwritten page of the history of our planet.

Another strong evidence, in corroboration of

Darwinist theories, is furnished by the Neolithic lake-dwellers. Geologists assert that the plants, found in the strata corresponding to the same period, were mainly of African origin, though discovered in Switzerland. They claim also to have found remains of looms, pottery, cereals, sheep, horses, etc.

Monsieur de Mortillet, professor of prehistoric anthropology in Paris, places man in the mid-Miocene period, and a number of learned men who have devoted years to this most interesting subject, have recognized the fact that a Miocene civilization once proven, it will upset entirely the stone-age period theory. No one has pleaded more earnestly for the archaic ages than the noted French writer Jacolliot. In his "Histoire des Vierges Les Peuples et les' Continents Disparus," he says: "Whatever may have been the place where a civilization more ancient than that of Greece, of Egypt, and of India was developed, it is certain that this civilization did exist, and it is highly important for science to recover its traces, however feeble and fugitive they be."

Hardly thirty years ago, the chronology of Egypt, India, and China was ridiculed, the limit to man's appearance on this earth being then irrevocably fixed at between six and seven thousand years Now, uncontrovertible testimony exists securing to the human race a place in the Miocene period, but it is refused admission into the Eocene age, thus far, though the soil produced vegetables and animals at the same geological epoch. We do not know how long it will take for science to determine, even approximately, the number of years contained in each period, but we do hope that when scientists proclaim such a fact, they will do it on an irrefutable basis.

CHAPTER II.

CONTINENTS.

"One generation passeth away and another cometh, but the earth abideth forever." Eccl., chap. I.

As the Romans adopted many customs from the Greeks, and were initiated by them into science and art, so their intellectual masters, the Greeks, had received from the Egyptians, through their sages, the knowledge which led them on the path of glory and fame. When Solon, towards the year 600 B. C., visited Egypt, he found that it was a very ancient country, already on its decline, with a long record of historical events; so long in fact that the Egyptian chronology was rejected as fabulous. Archæology and astronomy have united their efforts toward a solution of the question, with the startling effect of shaking up the conviction of the greatest bigots, and proving a few dates of great importance. Volney traced the Greek Zodiak back 16,984 years, but since he published his observations the famous Zodiak of Denderah has been demonstrated to be at least 80,000 years old; for it shows the passage of three sidereal years since it originated. The cause of the apparent contradictions in the chronology of the ancient civilized races lies simply in the different manner of reckoning; it is an effect of the prevalent ideas of the same epoch. For example, the year, *annus*, means heaven, revolution, and circle, and is closely related to religion and symbolism. History teaches us that some nations had adopted the apparent revolution of the sun in twenty-four hours, others the revolution of the moon in one month; others the interval of one solstice to another—or one season, calling each division by the generic name of revolution or year. But the knowledge of the sidereal year, or retrogradation of the sun, implies that the Egyptians knew astronomy to perfection. To have calculated that the sun with the starry heavens takes 25,868 years to return to the starting-point; in fact, to have become aware of the precession of the equinoxes, the old Egyptians must have been masters in mathematics, even when they erected their famous Denderah Zodiak, that is, nearly 80,000 years ago. When their civilization loomed up we do not know; tradition represents them always in possession of the greatest wisdom and knowledge that ever was on this earth. They claimed descent from the twelve "great gods," whom some authors think meant Poseidon, Cleito, and their ten sons. But there is another fact corroborating their descent from Atlantis. It is the mysterious celebration of the arrival of the thirteen great gods by the Aztec priesthood. The high civilization of the ancient Central American and Mexican races, so peculiarly like the Egyptian culture, the same knowledge of perfect astronomical reckoning as illustrated in the colossal Aztec calendar of the Cathedral of Santo Domingo (Mexico), point conclusively to the same origin. We must bear in mind that the Aztecs had been established in the city of Mexico only for a short period at the time of the landing of the Spaniards. They were barbarians compared to the Toltecs, Mayas, Quiches, and other great races, whose passage on the American continent can be traced through the grand ruins they have left scattered so promiscuously. Religious tenets had become horribly disfigured, but we can still trace the ancient Egyptian and Mexican symbols and legends to the same source. Sanchoniathon tells us that Kronos, King of Atlantis, visited the south and gave all Egypt to the god Taut, or Thoth, son of Misor, or Mestor, mentioned by Plato.

Now, the Quiche legends represent the mystic hero Votan as a legislator, and founder of mysteries. The ballet of the Xahoh-Tun, or sacred tapirs, was one of the principal features of the celebration of those mysteries. The magnificent ruins of the famous city called Zayi, testify to the present day to the mystic importance attached to the sacred dance of the Zayi, or Tapirs.

Furthermore, the Quiche manuscripts mention a very important fact, namely, that Votan brought the first tapirs (*perissodactyle*) to the Huehuetan River, where they multiplied rapidly, and where they are still to be found in large numbers. Geologists are unable to ascertain yet whether they existed in the Eocene period, but in deposits of Miocene date, remains, undistinguishable generically and specifically from the modern tapirs, have been found widely distributed all over the globe, extending even to France, Germany, and England, though they seem to have become extinct in Europe before the Pleistocene period. They abound still in two widely-separated regions of the earth, to wit, in Malaysia and in America, and in no intervening places. Another very strange fact to observe, is, that those closely allied animals have not undergone any amount of variation in forms during such an enormous period; and while, since the Miocene period, all other mammalian forms which existed, have either become extinct, or have undergone extensive modifications, tapirs have remained practically unchanged. It seems then very plausible to conclude that Votan's arrival in Central America could be easily traced to a period corresponding to the great cataclysm that submerged Atlantis; for tapirs have disappeared everywhere, they can be found at present only in an insignificant part of what belonged formerly to a lost continent, and in America, whither Votan imported them, most probably, from his Atlantean home.

Moreover, the venerable men who danced the ballet of the tapirs, carried a green palm in their hands, the emblematic twig, which Noah's dove also brought as a sign of a new period of manifestation of matter after a destructive cataclysm.

This is certainly a most remarkable coincidence, proving the common origin of two great prehistoric nations; who, though widely separated, agree still in their symbolism. But it would be erroneous to suppose that Atlantis or Poseidonis was only a great island; it was a great continent which did not disappear all at once, but sunk partly at different times; the last of all being the once-considered fabulous island of Atlantis. So that it does not appear strange that the inhabitants who escaped destruction should have located in opposite directions, and at an almost insuperable distance, because they were living at a remote distance from each other. It has been calculated that the famous island described by Plato, according to the description his ancestor Solon had obtained from the wise men of Sais, was submerged about 11,000 years ago. An occurrence, or rather phenomena, of that kind could not happen if it was not a natural law in the evolutionary phases of the earth. Lyell has remarked pertinently: "The connection between the doctrine of successive catastrophes and repeated deteriorations in the moral character of the human race, is more intimate and natural than might at first be imagined. For, in a rude state of society, all great calamities are regarded by the people as judgments of God on the wickedness of men. In like manner, in the account given to Solon by the Egyptian priests of the submersion of the island of Atlantis under the waters of the ocean, after repeated shocks of an earthquake, we find that the event happened when Jupiter had seen the moral depravity of the inhabitants." The vulgar loves always to see divine interference where there is really nothing but a natural phenomena. The whole universe is subject to the same cyclic law, which no power can change. We see everything undergoing a slow transformation because nothing is stationary. We follow an immense spiral with many curves, either ascending or descending, and always moving onwards impelled by a secret force, cyclic law.

How can we reconstrue the chronology of the ancient continents which have disappeared, is the problem of the present? Madame Blavatsky, in her last work, "The Secret Doctrine," says: "The final disappearance of the largest continent of Atlantis was an event coincident with the elevation of the Alps. It is on this colossal cataclysm, which lasted during a period of 150,000 years, that traditions of all the deluges are built, the Jews building their version on an event which took place later, in Poseidonis." This opinion is based on information furnished by occultists, and ought not to be disregarded because science has not yet approved of it. Geology mentions many deluges incomparably older, to wit, Paris, the gay capital of France, has been covered by the sea four times.

If we should wish, however, to illustrate still more forcibly the theory of the transformations which are constantly changing the face of the earth, we would refer to the fact that the bishop of Coutances, only a thousand years ago, used to go to the now island of Jersey, in a litter. It is also well known that the English sea, or channel, is eating up the French coast, and that it is only a question of time when Paris will be again on the floor of the Atlantic, slumbering for æons of ages previous to a re-awakening to light.

But it stands to reason that, if a whole continent could be sunk, other continents must have disappeared, while others will re-appear in future ages. We find on Easter Island traces of a civilization entirely different from the remains found either in Egypt, Chaldea, or Central America. It is not yet the artistic and cultured productions of a refined race like the Atlantean, but monstrous and cyclopean relics, like the giant statues found also in some parts of India. In the Lemurians we can discover the authors of many gigantic monuments, and trace to them all the legends of the different towers of Babel which were built by the Quinamés in Central America, and by the giants of the Mosaic flood in Asia. It is claimed that Africa is older than any other continent which is inhabited at present, and that America rose when Atlantis sunk. Is it then surprising to find the same types, legends, costumes, and traditions in Egypt and in Central America, the two widely separated nations which belonged once to the highly civilized Atlantean race? Of the Lemurians little is left, and still less known; but of their successors, the Atlanteans, we find remains widely spread, and admire in Grecian and Egyptian philosophy, science, and art, the cultured height to which they had soared. If Egypt was so grandly, so eminently superior when the Grecian sages considered her the acme of all centers of learning and wisdom, what was she at the apex of her glory? We can only answer, We could not teach them anything that they did not know, and we could learn a great deal from them.

Sir Charles Lyell, the father of geology, referring to the changes which occur periodically, says: " Respecting the cosmogony of the Egyptian priests, we gather much information from writers of the Grecian sects, who borrowed almost all their tenets from Egypt, and amongst others that of the former successive destruction and renovation of the world. We learn from Plutarch that this was the theme of one of the hymns of Orpheus, so celebrated in the fabulous ages of Greece. It was brought by him from the banks of the Nile, and we even find in his verses, as in the Indian systems, a definite period assigned for the duration of every successive world. The returns of great catastrophes were determined by the present period of the Magnus Annus, or great year, a cycle composed of the revolutions of the sun, moon, and planets, and terminating when these return together to the sign whence they were supposed at some remote epoch to set out. We learn particularly from the Timaeus of Plato that the Egyptians believed the world to be subject to occasional conflagrations and deluges. The sect of the Stoics adopted most fully the system of catastrophes destined at intervals to destroy the world. These, they taught, were of two kinds: the cataclysm or destruction by water, and the ecpyrosis, or destruction by fire or submarine volcanoes. From the Egyptians they derived the doctrine of the gradual debasement of man from a state of innocence. Toward the termination of each era the gods could no longer bear with the wickedness of man, and a shock of the elements, or a deluge, overwhelmed them; after which calamity Astrea again descended on the earth to renew the golden age."

In Genesis we find exactly the same theory expounded: "And God saw that the wickedness of man was great in the earth, and that every imagination of the thoughts of his heart was only evil continually—and, behold, I even I, do bring a flood of waters upon the earth, to destroy all flesh wherein is the breath of life, from under heaven; and everything that is in the earth shall die." This passage illustrates the cataclysm theory, and agrees with the traditions of almost every ancient race.

The ecpyrosis theory is obvious in the following

quotations: "For we 'will destroy this place, because the 'cry' of them is waxen great before the face of the Lord; and the Lord hath sent us to destroy it." "Then the Lord rained upon Sodom and upon Gomorrah brimstone and fire from the Lord out of heaven; and he overthrew those cities, and all the plain and all the inhabitants of the cities, and that which grew upon the ground." This legend in Genesis does not apply to only two cities, for wherefore are the words of Lot's daughter: "Our father is old, and there is not a man in the earth to come in unto us after the manner of all the earth; come let us make our father drink wine, and we will lie with him, that we may preserve seed of our father." Such words cannot certainly apply to one individual or his two daughters, but to the disappearance of one race and the dawn of another one. Thus it is claimed that Lemuria perished by fire, but Atlantis sunk to the bottom of the ocean.

We have archæological, ethnological, geological, traditional, botanical, and even biological evidences in support of the cyclic law which rules the periods of deterioration and restoration. In our own days the Sunda Island with 80,000 Malays sunk to the bottom of the Indian Ocean, and Greenland is losing ground so fast that no native will build by the sea-shore. Huxley has conclusively demonstrated that the British Islands have been submerged four times and then subsequently raised again, and consequently peopled each time with a new race, which must have come from some inhabited region. Madame Blavatsky in her last work says: "I believe in seven continents, four have disappeared, we live on the fifth, and two more will appear in the future." And again: "Patala, the Hindu name for America, antipodes of India, touched Atlantis. The Hindu Aryans knew the last surviving island of Atlantis which had perished soon after the upheaval of the two Americas. Thus America is older than Europe." It is also the reason why we find in India not only traces of Atlantean culture, but also a few relics of an older race, some gigantic remains of Lemuria, very scant it is true, but typical enough to insinuate a different epoch of disproportionate size in men, animals, plants, and monuments, such as would be suggested as having existed in Eocene and Miocene periods. It is, however, in Easter Island, that the greatest bulk of such cyclopean statues has been discovered.

Lyell relates a series of volcanic phenomena, earthquakes, troubled water, floating scoria, and columns of smoke, which have been observed at intervals since the middle of the last century, in a space of open sea between longitudes 20° and 22° west, about half a degree south of the equator. "These facts," says Mr. Darwin, "seem to show that an island or archipelago is in progress of formation in the middle of the Atlantic. A line joining St. Helena and Ascension would, if prolonged intersect this slowly nascent focus of volcanic action. Should land be eventually formed here, it will not be the first that has been produced by igneous action in this ocean since it was inhabited by the existing species of testacea. It would be difficult to estimate too highly the commercial and political importance which a group of islands might acquire if, in the next two or three thousand years, they should rise in mid-ocean between St. Helena and Ascension."

Donnelly quoting the same passage says: "These facts would seem to show that the great fires which destroyed Atlantis are still smouldering in the depths of the ocean; that the vast oscillations which carried Plato's continent beneath the sea may again bring it, with all its buried treasures, to the light; and that even the wild imagination of Jules Verne, when he described Captain Nemo, in his diving-armor, looking down upon the temples and towers of the lost island, lit by the fires of submarine volcanoes, had some groundwork of possibility to build upon." Sure enough, and if Atlantis should re-ascend to the surface of the ocean, as it will certainly in course of time, we might get considerable information from her remains concerning the Lemurian continent.

But what of the Hyperboreans? Who has not read of the incomparable climate that could be enjoyed in their country, which was sheltered from storms and wind; a blessed land from which originated tempests, storms, and wind, the producer of them, but not the sufferer of any discomfort from them. Herodotus bewails his inability to discover any traces of them. He wished to inquire about them from their neighbors, the Arimaspes, who, though they possessed only one eye, were very clear-sighted, but they were unable to furnish him with any information as to their whereabouts. Other authors well versed in ancient traditions give the name of Hyperborean to the Enchanted Islands, where the Hesperides kept watch over the famous golden apples. They were supposed to be situated in some secluded spot of the Occident.

The Greeks held in great veneration their two great national poems, the Iliad and Odysseus; and Homer's geography was the theme and subject of many debates among their sages and philosophers. They were as sacred to the Greeks as the Bible is to-day to the Christians; and many times twenty verses thereof furnished sufficient material for thirty books, because the text was emblematical.

On his voyage to the Arctic regions, the Swedish explorer Nordenskiold found fossils of horses, sheep, elephants, rhinoceroses, mammoths, etc., on a group of islands he discovered, which tends to credit the report of an inhabited Hyperborean continent where there are only glaciers now.

There are many allegories and ancient legends referring to the changes of climate in those distant times, when, from a frigid zone, the polar lands had become a country with a delightful temperature. Nearly all the gods of Egypt, Phœnicia, Greece, and many other Pantheons, are of a northern origin because formation is from north to south, and they were all embodying true facts relative to the history of the universe, or of mankind. Mythology illustrates the saying of Lefevre: "Nothing can save those that have run their course. It would be necessary to extend their cycle."

Tacitus, speaking of the Hyperborean continent, says: "As I am inclined to believe that the sun produces incense and aromatic plants in the East, I am convinced that at the point where he sets, the land being nearer to him, the earth exhales, on account of her proximity to him, those precious juices which go towards forming amber." It was only a repetition of the beautiful allegory sung by the ancient poets, in which they immortalized the golden tears shed by Apollo, at the death of his son Æsculapius, and the hot tears which Phæton's sisters dropped when they were informed of his untimely end. In both cases the tears were changed into amber, the Greek word *electron*, meaning the "stone of the sun." Now, the Grecian sages had said, a long time before Tacitus had mentioned it, that amber was an exhalation of the earth, which was produced and hardened by the sun, and that it was to be found in the Occident and in the North. It is well known that it is an exclusive product of northern seas, but principally of the Baltic. The myth, when properly interpreted, has reference to a change or rather transformation of the earth, and indicative of the antiquity of man. It is claimed by occultists that there is an eternal land at the North Pole, which they call the "White Island." They aver that it crowns the North Pole like a skull cap, and that it is subject to no changes whatever, remaining forever the same during the period of manifestation which is running its course. They consider the North Pole as the head of the earth, and the source of all beneficial action taken under an astral, or cosmical, point of view, while to the South Pole they attribute every lethal influence, for being the feet of the earth.

The following statement is authenticated by Mme. Blavatsky in her "Secret Doctrine:" The ancients made the polar circles seven instead of two, as Europeans do, for Mount Meru, which is the North Pole, is said to have seven gold and seven silver steps leading to it. The two poles are said to be the store-houses, the receptacles and liberators at the same time of cosmic and terrestrial vitality—electricity, from the surplus of which the earth, had it not been for these two natural safety-valves, would have rent to pieces long ago.

At the same time, it is now a new theory that has lately become an axiom, that the phenomena of polar lights is accompanied by, and productive of, strong sounds, like whistling, hissing, and cracking." The works of Trumholz on Aurora Borealis contain considerable information on the same subject.

Many scientists admit that formation runs from north to south, strengthening by that assertion the theory that the first continent was situated at the North Pole, while astronomically and allegorically the Celestial Pole, with its pole-star in heaven, is Meru among the Hindus; it is the seat of Brahma, as it was the throne of Jupiter. Typology begins with the constellation of Ursa Major, the primordial figure of the sacred number seven, the origin of numbers. With the pole-star of the Dragon are connected the greatest myths of archaic wisdom which we are recovering slowly in the ruined monuments of ancient races. Even the Greeks continued the traditions of past ages in their Hyperborean Apollo, and the fossils discovered by Nordenskiold seem to confirm the reality of a Hyperborean continent. It is also admitted by all naturalists that during the Miocene period, whether one or several million years ago, Greenland and Spitzbergen had almost a tropical climate; and occultists place their second or Hyperborean continent exactly in the same region.

CHAPTER III.
PAST, PRESENT, AND FUTURE RACES.

> "Necessity and chance approach me not,
> And what I will—is fate."

THE word "creation," as we understand it, with an anthropomorphic God, who has existed eternally in idleness, and who draws everything out of nothing, is so supremely ridiculous that it never entered the more rational conceptions of the ancients. Even the Hindus of our nineteenth century cannot comprehend such a ludicrous idea.

In a dialogue between the "Eternal Father" and the Superintendent of the Milky Way, Eugene Nus exclaims humorously: "There are, however, some people down below, who pretend that in your whole existence, you worked only one week, and that from the first Sunday on, you have remained with crossed arms, looking on." To this the Almighty answers: "It is easily understood that those people have not to fill up space. Who has been relating to them such fictions?"

"A man who pretends that you spoke to him from a burning bush."

"In my whole life I never spoke to anyone from any burning bush, but I do so through the voices of blackbirds and linnets, and I have never seen any fiery bush except in decorations of theaters.

That man has taken advantage of the innocence of his brethren. If they have invented many things like that about me, they must have conceived a very queer ideal of what I am on the superficie of yonder abortive planet."

And so it is. Our sun is only a third-class luminary, and the earth is neither the largest nor the best planet. It is not provided with such a beautiful system of rings as Saturn, or with as many satellites as either of the larger planets which move around our yellow sun. Our superiority exists only in our conceit, and while we know scientifically that not one inch of space can be called empty, it is reasonable to deduce that the universe existed before our earth was born into our present planetary system, and that it would continue to do so should our globe disappear now. The universe is boundless, limitless, and there is not a finger's breadth of void space anywhere, for matter is eternal, only it is forever undergoing transformations. We find a true system of cosmogenesis in ancient manuscripts that is common to every prehistoric nation. The same ideas abound in Hebraic Genesis, though the thick veil of symbolism that surrounds them has largely contributed towards misleading mankind. The Central American nations possessed an original Quiche document which is known under the name of manuscript of Chichicastenango. The same arrangement prevails in it. In every description relating to cosmic evolution, the narrator seems to be bent upon keeping back from the common herd the mysteries of the awakening of slumbering energies. Through the preconcerted darkness of the Quiche text, one can perceive the skillful hand of the priests of ancient times lowering the veil of symbolism upon the recital of the evolution of our planet. In the beginning no name is given to the Divinity; the formation of the universe, says the manuscript, proclaims the existence of a first cause, and is the incontestable proof of it. The immaculate One stands alone above the thoughts of the vulgar. They knew of Its existence, wise men worshiped It, but as It was formless and shapeless, no temple, no altar could be dedicated to It.

"O first and greatest God; by gods adored,
We own thy power, our Father and our Lord."
—*Iliad.*

"The Jews," says Rev. Robert Taylor, "had a superstition of not uttering the incomparable name of God." They had a good reason not to utter it, as they were not allowed to know it. Among the ancient nations it was a secret which was communicated only to the highest initiates, and even in Genesis, in the initial chapters, there is no such word as God, but the collective name Elohim is used throughout.

It is, however, in the philosophical schools of India that this system of an ever-existing principle is best expounded. The same doctrine is re-echoed by Hegel, who identifies absolute being or be-ness with non-being, and represents the universe as an eternal becoming. No one has ever given a better definition of the universal laws that rule the visible and invisible space than a sage of our present era : "The present is the child of the past, the future the begotten of the present, and yet, O present moment, knowest thou not that thou hast no parent, nor canst thou have a child; that thou art ever begetting but thyself? Before thou hast even begun to say, I am the progeny of the departed moment, the child of the past, thou hast become that past itself. Before thou utterest the last syllable, behold! thou art no more the present but verily that future! Thus are the past, the present, and the future the ever living trinity in one Mahamaya or the absolute Is."

In the Quiche cosmogony, we find conceptions conforming exactly with the teachings of the wisest inations: "Thus He was, when all was quiet and calm, when all was peaceful and silent, when nothing yet had stirred in the void of space. . . . The image of earth did not yet appear, the sea surrounded heaven, but all was shapeless, breathless, nothing was visible, all was motionless and peaceful, and amidst that infinite calm, only the indescribable One was. Dimly at first, a small speck appeared slowly moving on the boundless ocean. It assumed gradually the form of a boat, sailing towards an unknown region. Out of the pitch-like darkness came the fathers and generators wrapped in sky-blue robes, and they were named Gucumatz, which means serpent with dazzling azure wings; for they were illustrious sages, great scientific masters. They produced heaven, and but for them the "heart of heaven" exists. This agrees perfectly well with the theory of a central sun adopted by many occultists and philosophers, and partially recognized by scientists, who acknowledge that there must be a central point somewhere in the Milky Way. We find also a repetition of the doctrine of universal life, which was taught by the ancients, to which human mind is returning now, and which science is sullenly admitting by tracing its signs everywhere. It was Plato's "Anima Mundi," a doctrine as old as the world.

The central sun of the occultists, science has accepted astronomically, for it cannot deny the presence in sidereal space of a central body in the Milky Way, a point unseen and mysterious, the ever-hidden center of attraction of our sun and planetary system. While the western occultists and Jewish Kabalists claim that in this sun the Godhead is especially present, they accordingly refer to it the volitional acts of a Supreme Being, modeled upon the pattern furnished by theologians; the Eastern Initiates, however, take a different view of the subject. "They maintain," says a modern author, "that as the super-divine essence of the unknown Absolute is equally in every domain and place, the central sun is simply the center of universal life—electricity—the reservoir within which that divine radiance (already differentiated at the beginning of every creation) is focused. Though still in a laya, or neutral condition, it is, nevertheless, the one attracting, as also the ever-emitting, life center."

Now, if we accept the theory of universal life, we must admit the different creations mentioned in ancient manuscripts. In an old Mexican document four attempts at creating a perfect man are referred to; it is called the manuscript of Chimalpopoca. Among the Quiches, the attempts are only three, as enumerated in the manuscript of Chichicastenango. If we bear in mind that America and India drew their information from their Atlantean ancestors, we will not wonder at the coincidence of their traditions. "The ancients," says the Codex Chimalpopoca, "knew that in the year 1, Tochtli (Toltec and Aztec sacred chronology), the sky and earth had emerged out of chaos, and that, when it occurred thrice previously, life had been manifested on this planet, and man had appeared on earth for a fourth time. They also had an exact knowledge of the date corresponding to each periodical re-awakening, and used to claim that from "ashes God had formed man on the seventh day, but to Quetzalcohuatl they attributed the honor of producing a perfect human being."

The same idea is repeatedly expressed in the Kabala, in the "Book of Concealed Mystery," in the "Greater Holy Assembly," and in the "Lesser Holy Assembly." Those fruitless attempts at creating a perfect physical man are recorded in the passages describing the appearance and disappearance of the Edomite kings: "And there are kings which have reigned in ADVM, Edom. In the land of Edom; that is in the place wherein all judgments exist." Here we feel bound to remind the reader that the science of Gematria, or first division of the so-called literal Kabala, is based on the correspondence between words and numbers, and their relative numerical value, each Hebrew letter representing also a quantity. Thus, in the above quotation, the sense of the sentence is contained in the word $ADVM = 1+4+6+40 = 51 = Na = $ Failure. Na, being synonymous with 51, expresses pain, and also unbalanced force, which is the source of failure. Consequently the seven Edomite kings refer to the prior worlds as well as to the first races.

"And because that constitution of Adam was not as yet found, they could not subsist nor be conformed, and they were destroyed. Have they then been abolished, and are all these included? For truly they were abolished that they might be withdrawn from form until there should come forth the representative of Adam." We could quote extensively from the books of the Kabala concerning the subject of prior worlds and early earthly races,. which were only expressions of unbalanced force, but we will end our digression by stating that our race began, according to kabalistical reckonings, when the sun entered the sign of the Bull having in opposition the Scorpion, which embodies the symbol of the generative principle. It was followed by the Balance when the sun entered the zodiacal division of the Ram.

In the Quiche manuscript we find the following version: "After having brought forth the earth, with its mountains, forests, and seas, and having replenished them with animals of all species, the gods, who accompanied the blue-feathered serpent, proceeded to the formation of man, but twice they failed in their undertaking. In their first attempt they brought out a man of clay, a fragile, worthless thing, who melted under the first shower of rain. Disgusted with their first offspring, the creators abandoned him to his fate, without giving up their self-imposed task. It becomes apparent that they realized that a more substantial creature alone could withstand the climatic changes which our planet was undergoing. Consequently they met with such insuperable obstacles in their endeavor to form a being suitable to existing conditions, that they required the assistance of two powerful chiefs of the magic art. The latter responded promptly to the call of their masters; they traced lines and circles, they scattered grains of corn and pieces of *dogwood* (or tzite) around, they addressed invocations to the sun, and behold! a wooden man appeared followed by a cibak woman, *i. e.*, made of the marrow of the iris (reed). While creating these new beings, the gods had intended to correct the defects of the race that was modeled out of clay, yet they failed again. Those wooden men looked stiff; they had neither blood, fat, nor fluidic element; they were ungraceful; their complexion was sallow; their hands and feet were dried up; and though they were endowed with a tongue, they lacked intelligence. They propagated their species so rapidly that the whole earth was soon swarming with beings who resembled them. They were so ungrateful that they brought upon them the wrath of their divine makers, whom they forgot as soon as they came out of their hands. Therefore, they were doomed to destruction. A burning shower of bitumen and resin rained upon them. However, this ill-fated race did not entirely perish, because the celestial creators wished to preserve a small number of them, to perpetuate the remembrance of the wooden men they had generated. They live now in woods and forests, and are known to us under the name of apes."

The passage describing the emerging of the human race at the dawn of the third creation begins as follows: "Here we must consider man and what could compose his flesh, for so far he had none." If we admit the immortality of the soul, or rather that something, whatever its name may be, survives our body, that something must have always been in existence, at least in essence, or it would perish, on the principle that what has a beginning must have an end. "The universe," says a modern philosopher, "is not an effect, it is the cause of all effects; every being it contains is the necessary effect of this cause, which sometimes shows us its manner of acting, but generally conceals its operations. Men use the word chance to hide their ignorance of true causes, which, though not understood, act not less according to certain laws. There is no effect without a cause. Nature is a word used to denote the immense assemblage of beings, various matter, infinite combinations, and diversified motions that we behold. All bodies organized or unorganized are necessary effects of certain causes. Nothing in nature can happen by chance. Everything is subject to fixed laws. These laws are only the necessary connection of certain effects with their causes. One atom of matter cannot meet another by chance; this meeting is the effect of permanent laws, which cause every being necessarily to act as it does, and hinder it from acting otherwise, in given circumstances To talk of the fortuitous concourse of atoms, or to attribute some effects to chance, is merely saying that we are ignorant of the laws by which bodies act, meet, combine, or separate. If we substitute the words divine interference for chance, we have an irresistible argument in favor of an ever-existing principle, which we are all agreed to call matter." Such argument, if adopted as a fact, would become the death-blow to all special creation theories, and render it absolutely necessary to admit the existence of lost continents and diversified races. It would strengthen the belief founded upon hoary traditions, of human species differently framed from our historical generations, and endowed with qualities not pertaining to our present races. Geologists have forcibly demonstrated the transformations that the animal kingdom has undergone from the Eocene period; but anthropologists have done less towards clearing up the mystery that surrounds man's early existence. Professor Baumgartner says: "The first men who proceeded from the germs of animals beneath them, lived first in a larva state." The point is essentially important but not thoroughly true, because it has not been proven yet whether man was first to appear on earth, or animals preceded him. Occultists assure us that human beings were evolved before their dumb brothers, and that the latter were the result of man's cast-off tissues. They give us a very plausible story of the early races, and allow us a glimpse into the mysterious records of by-gone ages. In the Kabala, and in the Eastern philosophical works, we find an elaborate system in which man emanates from a group of seven celestial men. The same idea permeates the first chapter of Genesis, in which Elohim (not

God as translated) is the principal actor: "And Elohim said: 'Let there be light; and there was light.'" It means simply that the first race was composed of ethereal beings, spiritual, but lacking the intelligence which had to be acquired through a long course of training upon our little planet, earth. There was no sex discernible, in either animals or men, and they developed monstrous bodies which were adapted to their coarse surroundings. As light was the first wish expressed by Elohim, so sight must have been the first sense which men acquired in the early period, when they were generated by the divine creators, as expressed in the Quiché text. At the close of what the Buddhists call the first round, man must have become more material, thus falling surely, though slowly, into generation. Of that first race, science cannot identify any remains in the lower strata of the Primordial epoch, for there are none. How long man retained a sufficiency of his spiritual nature to control matter, is hard guess-work. Traditions and legends remember only the epoch when he had developed a gigantic stature, and had become an enemy of his own spiritual ancestors. In the Greek Theogony, Gæa, the earth, unites herself to Uranus or heaven, and begets the first gods, better known under the names of Cyclopes, Titans and Centimanes. Prompted by their mother they conspire against their father, and induce Kronos, the youngest and bravest of them, to lay violent hands on Uranus. In Genesis, a story somewhat similar to the pagan version is related in chapter vi: "There were giants in the earth in those days; and also after that, when the sons of God came in unto the daughters of men, and they bare children to them, the same became mighty men which were of old, men of renown." Hesiod records, also, the tradition about the men of the age of bronze (the admixture of two metals being very significant), whom Jupiter had made out of ashwood, and who had hearts harder than diamonds. Clad in bronze from head to foot, they passed their lives fighting. So was one of the Central American races made out of wood, and so were their giants proud and overbearing. Thus, we find a popular belief among the ancients resting on a truthful basis.

Madame Blavatsky, the expounder of the occultist's doctrines, avers that the men of the third race were the ancestors of the Atlanteans. They were just such ape-like, intellectually senseless, giants as were those beings who, during the third period, represented humanity. Morally irresponsible, it was these third-race men who, through promiscuous connection with animal species lower than themselves, created the missing link, which became, ages later (in the tertiary period) only, the remote ancestor of the real ape, as we find it now, in the pithecoid family. Again we find occult docrines agreeing with ancient legends as preserved in the Quiche manuscript: "However the whole race did not entirely perish, the divine creators preserved a small number of those ungrateful beings in memory of the wooden men they had generated. They live now in woods and forests, and are known to us by the name of apes." This theory dissents from Darwinism surely, but it has been eagerly caught by some men of science. Among them a well-known Hanoverian is showing with great ingenuity that Darwin was wholly mistaken in tracing man back to the ape. On the contrary, he maintains that it is the ape which is evolved from man. This is a purely Brahmanic, Buddhistic, and Kabalistic, philosophy resting on the inevitable law of necessity, which rules in every manifestation of matter, and governs the growth and decadence or degeneration of every race. If we consider the truthful assertion that the earth began by being a liquid ball of fire, a protoplasmic phantom of what it is now, we must conclude that man must have followed the course of his mother, and have been also a fiery ball, which acquired solidity in the course of time. It is rational to deduce therefore that he was sexless at first, developed into an androgynous being, and at last separated into male and female. According to the Hindu calendar, the separation of sexes occurred 18,618,728 years ago.

The third race is called by the occultists the "Sons of passive Yoga," because it was produced unconsciously by the second race, which, because it was intellectually inactive, is supposed to have been constantly plunged in a kind of blank or abstract contemplation, as required by the conditions of the Yoga state. How quickly they progressed materially and intellectually can be only surmised if we accept the traditions of occultism, which depict the Lemuro Atlantean of the closing third race as a highly civilized individual. That during the early geological periods men built large cities, cultivated arts and sciences, possessed a knowledge of natural laws which we are only recovering slowly, and were experts in astronomy and mathematics, is incontrovertible. The further we push our researches, the more convincing the argument becomes. Take, for example, the "Book of Nabathean Agriculture." Dr. Chwolson agrees with Quatremere that it contains no trace of Christianity, or of the existence of Arsacian, Selucian, and Sassanidan rule. Twenty Babylonian kings are enumerated in the Agriculture, and of these twenty names, there is not one which coincides with that of a king of any known Babylonian dynasty. In separating into their respective classes the quotations which are mingled together in the Agriculture, the finds at Babylon a rich and varied literature, fully equal to that which was developed among the Greeks several thousand years later. All the sages mentioned are priests, founders of religions, moralists, naturalists, astronomers, agriculturists, and are universally endeavoring to introduce a worship freed from idolatrous superstitions.

Now the word Nabathean comes from Nebo, the deity of the planet Mercury, and the god of Wisdom Mercury, was also Hermes; thus Nebo, Mercury and Hermes represent the same idea, and link three great nations of ancient times closely together. Their reimains disclose no nascent civilization; on the contrary, they exhibit an uninterrupted line of evidences tending to prove that they enjoyed all the benefits of highly cultured nations, but the origin thereof is lost in the night of time.

In Hesiod's "Theogony," we find the evolution of the human race from a spiritual plane down to our present physical state graphically described and the history of the growth and disappearance of the continents on which men thrived, is fully recorded. As Uranus destroyed his children from Gaia by confining them in the bosom of the earth, Tythea, so Kronos, at the second stage of creation, destroyed his children from Rhea by devouring them; an allusion to the fruitless efforts of nature to produce real human men, which we have previously quoted from the Quiche text. Then comes Zeus Jupiter, who dethroned his father, the same disrespectful son found in every cosmogony. He is described by Hermes as the Heavenly Man or Pymander, and by Moses under the name of Adam and Ham.

Uranus is the Varuna of the Hindus; it embodies the grandest conception of Archaic races, and is synonymous with the Cœlum of the Latins, or a vault, a hollow, a concave extension, which unites with the earth, or Terra. The latter word is derived from the past participle *Tersa* (the dry element), in opposition to *mare*, the wet element, and reveals the fundamental basis of the Mosaic Genesis, and of every cosmogony, and the principal structure of all religions, in their primeval phases of heavenly and earthly dualities. "It takes earth and water to create a human soul," says Moses. Adam, Jehovah, Brahma, and Mars are in one sense identical, because they are all symbols of primitive or initial generative powers for the purpose of human procreation. The word Adam means red, and so does Brahma—Viraj—while the planet Mars is depicted red by astronomers, and the god Mars, as well as Jehovah, was the god of war and bloodshed. Water is understood to be the blood of the earth, and the names of the deities connected with the divine generators of mankind are synonymous with either earth or water. Mars is identical with Kartiktya, who in one sense is the god of war of the Hindus, and was born of the sweat of Siva and the earth. In the Mahabharata, he is shown as born without the intervention of a woman, and he is called "Lohita," the red, like Adam and the other "first men." Hence, the author of the "Source of Measure" is quite right in thinking that Mars, and all the other gods of like attributes, being the gods of war and of bloodshed, were the outgrowth of a secondary idea flowing out of the primary

PAST, PRESENT, AND FUTURE RACES. 59

one of shedding blood in conception, for the first time. Hence, Jehovah became later a fighting god, "Lord of Hosts," and one who commanded war. Plato states that the deity geometrizes in fabricating the universe, and his assertion is corroborated in the Sepher—Jesirah—or numbers of creation, in which the whole process of evolution is given out in numbers. In its "32 paths of Wisdom," the number 3 is repeated four times and the number 4 five times. Therefore the wisdom of the creating powers is contained in numbers. The word sepher or seph-ra, when unvoweled, means to cipher: "And Alhim (31,415 to 1) said: Let there be light (20,612 to 6,561). In the Zohar and the Sepher Jesirah, the archaic doctrines could have been traced back to their original sources, but what was left of them was subsequently embodied in the Pentateuch proper, and especially in Genesis. The latter contains sublime pages referring to the manifestation of matter in its secondary stage, but theogony is left out, and the word God is certainly not mentioned in the initial chapters of Genesis, the collective name of Elohim being used throughout in the original text. "And Elohim said: Let us make man in our image, after our likeness: and let them have dominion over the fish of the sea, and over the fowl of the air, and over the cattle, and over all the earth, and over every creeping thing that creepeth upon the earth." "So Elohim created man in his own image, in the image of Elohim created he him; male and female created he them." This passage is constantly misconstrued, for it does not refer to our present supremely material race, but to the Heavenly Man of the Kabalists, the collective group of celestial men of the occultists, the companions of the "Azure Winged Serpent" of the Quichés, the gods, creators, and generators of the human race. "Male and female created he them," does not refer to one single man, but to many, emanating from their divine prototypes and endowed with the power of reproducing their species. They were androgynous, as stated so explicitly in the passage just quoted. This first man is the Sephirothal Host of the Kabalists, and is entirely different from the Adam of the second chapter. That it must have been an etherial being is conclusively deduced by the second chapter, in which we find an unanswerable sentence: "And every plant of the field before it was in the earth, and every herb of the field before it grew: for the Lord God had not caused it to rain upon the earth, and there was not a man to till the ground," is a flat contradiction to the hypothesis that the man of the first chapter was a human being, with flesh and bone. He was, on the contrary, a shadow, an astral form, like the plants and animals which were following the same course of evolution delineated by his prototypes, and the earth itself was still a fluidic mass. "But there went up a mist from the earth and watered the whole face of the ground." Here we can notice the first initiatory step toward materializing the earth and everything thereon, and the second Adam appears. He is not modeled at the likeness of Elohim: "And Elohim formed man of the dust of the ground, and breathed into his nostrils the breath of life; and man became a living soul." As we understand that Elohim here represents the three lowest spiritual beings of the Sephirothal Host, we may infer that, while one of them made earthly Adam of dust, the other breathed into him the breath of life, and the third one made him a living soul, all of which is implied in the plural number of Elohim. The being thus evolved is still mindless, non-intelligent. It is only in the third Adam, the one in which the sexes separate, that the rebellion of matter against spirit becomes manifest. That they were both naked, and were not ashamed, proves their innocence, and their lack of intelligence.

Adam is the personification of a dual being,—the Creator, a celestial being, and his progeny, the terrestrial Adam, who had only *nephesh*, "the breath of life," and received a living soul into his material body after his fall. Thus, the word Adam was a form of universal symbol, which, even among the Jews, indicated four distinct races: 1. An ethereal, shadowy spiritual man. 2. A protoplastic, androgynous being. 3. An innocent Adam, made of dust. 4. The fallen Adam, progenitor of our own race.

That men were evolved at first without being begotten, and had to develop the five senses we possess now successively, according to the immutable laws that govern this universe, we cannot doubt. We may be assured also that during the immense geological periods required for the solidification of the earth, beings analogous to her extant condition swarmed in her bosom, and on her surface, as they do now. What keeps mankind plunged into abject ignorance, is the double sense of sacred writings. Eschylus, author of the Trilogy and "Prometheus Bound," was condemned to be stoned to death, being charged with sacrilege by the Athenians for revealing the mysteries. In every age, it has been dangerous to depart from prejudices consecrated by opinion. All that the most enlightened men could do was to speak ambiguously, though, from a base complaisance, they often mix falsehood with truth. Several had a double doctrine, one public and the other secret, and as no key was available except to initiates, their true sentiments have become unintelligible, and have given rise to all theological doctrines.

CHAPTER IV.

THE SACRED SCRIPTURES.

"In contemplation if a man begin with certainties, he will end in doubts; but if he will be content to begin with doubts, he shall end in certainties."—*Bacon.*

"THE highest honor we can pay to truth is to show our confidence in it, and our desire to have it sifted and analyzed by how rough a process soever; as being well assured that it is that alone that can abide all tests, and which, like the genuine gold, will come out all the purer from the fiercer fire." (Rev. Robert Taylor, in "Diegesis.") Symbology is so thoroughly linked with mythology, whether ancient or archaic, that a knowledge of both is requisite to become conversant with the primitive way of conveying ideas, and as mythology was the origin of every religious tenet extant in the world, we will trace presently our own Christian doctrine back to its true source. There is a natural connection between all religions, and there is one also between all languages; both are the result of cycles of evolution, they are the outgrowth of a primitive germ, lost in the night of time. To suppose that our Christian religion was the result of a special revelation with no reliable evidence to corroborate such an assertion, is to build on a sandy foundation. No nation ever made such a pretense in antiquity, except a hybrid race, the Jews, who, even in religious matters, were the old-clothes men of the world. Whatever they gathered from the neighboring nations on cosmogony and theology does not show any real mark of improvement. The Orientalists, Egyptologists, and Assyriologists have discovered, one by one, every Hebraic legend which was claimed to be unique or original, in the recovered documents of prehistoric races. The pious Sir William Jones concludes his "Asiatic Researches" with the following sentences: "Thus have I attempted to trace, with a confidence, continually increasing as I advanced, a parallel between the gods adored in Greece, Italy, and India; but which was the original system, and which the copy, I will not presume to decide. I am persuaded, however, that a connection existed between the old idolatrous nations of Egypt, India, Greece, and Italy, long before the birth of Moses." The great Orientalist leaves the reader without expressing his own conclusion, because, undoubtedly, "too much light is hurtful to the eyes."

The oldest religions in the world, known at present, are the Indian, Mazdean, and Egyptian. They were established on the same basis, as proven by their sacred Scriptures,—the Vedas of the Hindus, the Zend Avesta of the Parsees, the Book of the Dead, and the Ritual of the Egyptians,—and none can be understood without a previous knowledge of symbology. Then comes the Chaldean religion next. It is known generally under the disfigured phase of Sabeism, as interpreted by archæologists who have recovered the "Book of Numbers," the Assyrian tiles, and four books belonging to the collection called, singularly enough, "The Nabathean Agriculture." This last work allows us a faint glimpse into the realm of Chaldean philosophy. From the Egyptian and Babylonian systems the Jews derived their Bible, which is undoubtedly the youngest Scripture claiming divine inspiration, if we except the Koran, or Book of God. The latter appeared last, and had the best opportunity for plagiarism.

The application of chronology to matters of faith is exhibited nowhere except in the Jewish Bible, and it does not redound to the credit of its authors. Anterior to King David's reign, there is no data of any reliable historian which confirms one single fact related in the Old Testament. The Jewish historian Josephus lived about sixty years after the date attributed to Jesus' apparition, or incarnation on earth, and his works are constantly brought forward as authoritative. He sought vainly for the testimony of Egyptian authors to support the pretensions he advanced concerning the antiquity of the Hebrews. Not one of them has so much as mentioned the prodigies of Moses, or held out the least glimpse of probability, or coincidence to his romantic tale. The drowning of a Pharaoh with his whole army would certainly have been recorded in the annals of a people, that has left us so many imperishable mementoes of its past, but not a single fact has ever been discovered, among the historical relics of any of the Hebrew contemporaries, corroborating their historical Bible previous to holy King David. The whole fable of Moses, however, is to be found in the Orphic verses sung in the orgies of Bacchus, as celebrated in Egypt, Syria, Asia Minor, and Greece, ages before such people as the Jews were known to be in existence. The Chaldean tablets give the allegorical description of creation, the fall, the flood, and the tower of Babel, with the history of Moses. How can the Pentateuch be called a revelation? The tower of Babel especially was a myth very widely spread, even in America, ages before the landing of the Spaniards. In a work translated by Fray Diego Duran, in 1579, called "History of New Spain," and deposited in the Royal Library of Madrid, the version of it is: "After they had raised it so high that it reached the sky, the Lord of the Divine Heights said to the inhabitants of heaven: 'Have you noticed how the inhabitants of the earth have built such a high and superb tower to ascend here, because they are enticed hither by the beauty and brightness of the sun? Come, let us confound them, for it is not just that those who live on the earth, and are in the flesh, should mix with us.' Instantly the inhabitants of the skies rushed from the four corners of the world, and like lightning destroyed the building which men had raised; whereupon the terror-stricken giants were separated and scattered on all sides of the earth."—*Chap. 1, Vol. 1.*

None better than the Jews knew that a hidden meaning was underlying the text of the first books of the Bible, for the keys to it are concealed in some secret philosophical works called the Kabala, which, like their theology, was nothing more than the Oriental philosophy plagiarized, and remodeled to suit their own conceit. In the course of their ramblings into the adjacent countries of Egypt, Assyria, and Phœnicia, they could not help learning the tenets of the doctrines of those nations. "One thing, indeed," says the great ecclesiastical writer, Mosheim, "appears at first sight very remarkable—that the variety of religions and gods in the heathen world neither produced wars nor dissensions among the different nations." Certainly it did not, for learned men allege, with the most convincing arguments, that the principal deities of all the Gentiles resembled each other in their essential characters, and that their being worshiped under different names could not bring any confusion into mythology, since they were all derived from the same source; a fact demonstrated by symbology most conclusively." "The various modes of worship which prevailed in the Roman world," says Gibbon, "were all considered by the people as equally true—by the philosophers as equally false, and by the magistrates as equally useful.

"Both the interests of the priests and the credulity of the people were sufficiently respected. In their writings and conversation the philosophers of antiquity asserted the independent dignity of reason; but they resigned their actions to the commands of law and custom. Viewing with a smile of pity and indulgence the various errors of the vulgar, they diligently practiced the ceremonies of their fathers, devoutly frequented the temples of the gods, and sometimes, condescending to act a part on the theater of superstition, they concealed the sentiments of an atheist under the sacerdotal robe. Reasoners of such a temper were scarcely inclined to wrangle about their respective modes of faith, or of worship. It was indifferent to them what shape the folly of the multitude might choose to assume; and they approached with the same inward contempt and the same external reverence to the altars of the Lydian, the Olympian, or the Capitoline Jupiter." Gibbon's elegant account of the matter is only partially true, for the very institution of the mysteries is an eloquent answer to an accusation of atheism at large, or of popular folly. Mythology is the imperishable book in which nature has written in indelible characters a priceless record, the history of mankind on the little planet earth. The ancients knew it so well that they gave manifold meanings to their symbolical gods, and wrapped their sacred writings with such an impenetrable veil of mystery, that they remained sealed books to the ignorant people, and will remain so for many years to come.

In the "Lesser Mysteries" all that was historical and interpretative was communicated to the neophytes, but the "Greater Mysteries" were reserved for those whose spiritual unfoldment entitled them to the knowledge of truth, and the secret workings of nature. From the Egyptians down to the Jews, the correct measure of time was considered such a great secret, that, to reveal it to uninitiated persons, was considered as a most heinous sin. Moreover, the Hebrews taught that to divulge the Rabbinical mysteries to any outsider, or impart to them the secrets contained in the Kabala, was like eating of the fruit of the Tree of Knowledge; it was punishable by death. How then can the Christian gospel teachers pretend to explain the Bible to small children? It seems almost too ludicrous to be believed, when one knows that without the key to it, the Old Testament is incomprehensible. The sacred books of all the ancient nations require another book to be interpreted by, and as the Hebrews concealed the key to their Holy Scriptures in the Kabala, the Hindus hid the one to their Vedas in the Upanishads. Cowell has remarked very pertinently that "the Upanishads breathe an entirely different spirit from other Brahmanical writings," they bear an expression of thought unknown in any earlier work, except the Rig Veda hymns. When truly interpreted, the Vedas, the Zend Avesta, and the Jewish Bible will revolutionize the world; they will be the death of those false theologies, built upon ignorance and falsification. They were unwittingly the cause of the evil; in their true interpretion lies the remedy. Read by the light of the Zohar, the initial four chapters of Genesis, which have been criticised so severely, become a highly philosophical fragment in the history of the world's cosmogony, and agree thoroughly with the records kept by many other nations, and on other continents, *i. e.*, America. The Pentateuch is a collection of allegorical legends, not always a suitable reading for youth. In their symbolical garb they are a myth, a nursery tale, a monstrous attempt to play havoc with science and logic, an evident effect of the spite of Jehovah's followers. To have let them serve as a prologue to Christianity was the greatest error committed by the early Fathers of the church, who knew very well what the Pentateuch meant, and who appropriated it against the wishes of the Rabbis. The latter exercised the severest vengeance by allowing the Christians to remain in possession of the dead letter, while they kept the secret meaning to themselves.

Christianity, however, is not connected so absolutely with the Jewish religion as to owe it its existence. On the contrary, many of the shrewder advocates of the present system have expressed frequently their desire that the two doctrines should be considered independent of each other. "The law was given by Moses, but grace and truth came by Jesus Christ," says John; and then again, "All that ever came before me are thieves and robbers," quoting Christ's own words to his apostles when referring to the old dispensation. We agree with the apostle's last sentence, so we will proceed to consider if the New Testament can stand any more sifting down than Judaism.

It has been asserted frequently that Jesus belonged to a sect called Essenes (Matthew ii, 23): "That it might be fulfilled which was spoken by the prophet, He shall be called a Nazarene," that is a Therapeut (Epiphanius). Eusebius, an early church Father of great authority among Christians, claims that the monastic life was derived from the Essenes, and Epiphanius asserts that the Nazarenes and the Nazarites of the Old Testament were members of the same sect. We read in Basnage's "Histoire des Juifs:" "Matthew ii, 23, 'That it might be fulfilled which was spoken by the prophets, he shall be called a Nazarene;' that is (as we see from Epiphanius), a Therapeut. It is certain that none of the Jewish prophets had so said. Some other equally sacred writings are referred to, though their accomplishment by the mere resemblance of the name of the city in which

Jesus is said to have resided, to that of the order of monks to which he was believed to have belonged, is a most miserable pun. The Jews, however, who think it reasonable to admit that such a person as Jesus really existed, place his birth nearly a century sooner than the generally assumed epoch." The word era is derived from the four initial letters of the formula, "Ab Exordio Regni Augusti," which means, "from the beginning of the reign of Augustus," and for several centuries after the establishment of Christianity, nations continued to reckon from the starting-point they had adopted, evincing the greatest indifference as to the year in which Jesus Christ was born. A very obscure monk, by the name of Dyonisius Exiguus or the Little, calculated, by the means of chronological tables, the year of the birth of Jesus Christ. He lived in the year 580 at Rome, but his contemporaries paid little attention to his discovery, and it was only two centuries afterwards, that the venerable Bede exhorted the Christians to adopt it, and Carlos Magnus in 800 issued an edict legalizing it.

We read in the "Acts" that the disciples were first called Christians at Antioch, and the learned Jesuit Nicolaus Serarius contends that the first Christian monks were Essenes. Anyhow, it cannot be denied that the most eminent Fathers of the church had been educated and trained in the University of Alexandria. Furthermore, the most valued manuscripts of the New Testament are

Codices Alexandrini. Here it becomes necessary to investigate the character and origin of that most remarkable set of men, the Essenes, on account of the prominent part they played in the origination and production of the Christian Scriptures. The most celebrated writers of antiquity, such as Philo, Josephus, Pliny, and Solinus, have mentioned them frequently under the name of Therapeuts or Essenes, which means the same thing, the only difference being that Essene is an Egyptian word, and Therapeutæ is Greek, but they are synonymous with Surgeons, Healers, and Curates.

"It was in Egypt," says the great ecclesiastical historian, Mosheim, "that the morose discipline of Asceticism took its rise; and it is observable, that that country has in all times, as it were by an immutable law or disposition of nature, abounded with persons of a melancholy complexion, and produced, in proportion to its extent, more gloomy spirits than any other parts of the world. It was here that the Essenes dwelt principally, *long before the coming of Christ."—Vol. 1, p. 196.*

Quoting the same author, Rev. Robert Taylor says: "It is not the first glance, nor cursory observance, that will sufficiently admonish the reader of the immense historical wealth put into his hand, by this stupendous admission, this surrender of the key-stone of the mighty arch,—this giving up of everything that can be pretended for the evidences of the Christian religion."

This admission of the great ecclesiatical historian (than whom there is no greater), will serve us as the Pythagorean theorem—the great geometrical element of all subsequent science, of continued recurrence, of infinite application—ever to be borne in mind, always to be brought in proof—presenting the means of solving every difficulty, and the clue for guiding us to every truth: "Bind it about thy neck, write it upon the tablet of thy heart"—everything of Christianity is of Egyptian origin.

The Therapeuts, or Essenes, are also recognized by that great pillar of the church, the famous historian Eusebius, who acknowledges them as Christians, and who declares most emphatically that their ancient writings were our *own Gospels and Epistles*. After such a confession, no argument would be of any avail if we prove, once for all, how the Christian world became possessed of the New Testament. In the year 327 A. D., the Grand Council of Nice, in Bythinia, took place under the presidency of Constantine the Great. Pappus, in his Syndicon to the same council, affirms that, "having placed all the sacred books under the altar in a church, the Fathers besought the Lord that during the night the inspired writings might get upon the altar, and the spurious ones remain underneath. The next morning they repaired to the sacred edifice, and found on the altar our New Testament, or rather the books of which it is composed, and they rejected those that had remained underneath. The

Romans used to have a maxim: "The common people like to be deceived—let them be deceived (*Vulgus vult decipi—decipiatur*)," and so it has been with the Christian world at large.

The immediate effect of the introduction of Christianity was absolutely disastrous. It seems as though man's understanding had collapsed entirely. A dark age was ushered upon the smoldering ashes of Grecian and Roman monuments. To a golden era wonderfully fertile in orators, philosophers, and artists, succeeded a generation of barbarians unable to understand the genius that guided their more highly gifted predecessors. Neither did virtue reign. From the beginning, the church Fathers, and even the apostles, deplore the corruption that is infecting all ranks. "Were a wise man," says Bishop Kidder, "to choose his religion by the lives of those who profess it, perhaps Christianity would be the last religion he would choose." The reason lies in the system adopted by the philosophical schools and theological teachers, that "there are many truths which it is useless for the vulgar to know." Strabo shows, at great length, the general use of double meaning in theogony and sacred writings, and their important effects. Euripides maintained that in the early state of society, wise men insisted on the necessity of darkening truth, and persuading men of the existence of an ever present immortal deity who hears, sees, and understands our actions, though we may think differently ourselves. The most distinguished legislators of antiquity were ardent advocates of that system, which we find underlying every religious doctrine of prehistoric races. It is illustrated in the legends and traditions of the ancient Central American races, in the Chaldean tablets, in the Greek mythology, in the Egyptian papyrus, in the Druidic dolmen, in the Parsee and Hindu sacred books. No wonder that the Bible is written in the same spirit, and is so misconstrued in spite of all the warnings repeated so frequently. "And the disciples came and said unto him, Why speakest thou unto them in parables? He answered and said unto them, Because it is given unto you to know the mysteries of the kingdom of heaven, but to them it is not given." Matt. xiii, 10. Surely here, and in innumerable passages to the same effect, we find the mystical-sense system of the Therapeuts fully exemplified; and the same allegorical method of expounding their scriptures, so characteristic of the Egyptian monks, we find thoroughly adopted by Paul, in his Epistle to the Galatians, chap. iv: "For it is written, that Abraham had two sons, the one by a bondmaid, the other by a free woman. But he who was of the bondwoman was born after the flesh; but he of the free woman was by promise. Which things are an allegory; for these are the two covenants; the one from the Mount Sinai which gendereth to bondage, which is Agar. For this Agar is Mount Sinai in Arabia,

THE SACRED SCRIPTURES. 77

and answereth to Jerusalem which now is, and is in bondage with her children. But Jerusalem which is above is free, which is the mother of us all."

We could quote extensively to illustrate a fact establishing the irrefutable evidence of the Egyptian origin of all that is called Christian. Even the sacraments were patched up in the vacuum left by the deserted mysteries. During the second century after the introduction of Christianity, the church fathers, being well aware of the deep respect entertained by Greeks and Romans alike for their "mysteries," resolved to give to their religion the same seal of mysticism, with the hope of putting the pagan and Christian creeds on the same footing. They instituted sacraments, plagiarizing from the heathen not only the terms, but even the empty rites, of the desecrated mysteries, and adorning with pompous formulas and solemn titles, ceremonies which to the ignorant masses soon became a meaningless superstition. They adopted also the Oriental method of teaching their religion with symbols, images, signs, and even actions, which in course of time lost entirely their original significance. The chasm which separated paganism from Christianity has been bridged over again by erudition. Science has re-united all the races that lived on this little planet, earth, by establishing the irrefutable fact of the common origin of all religions; thus proving that they were all derived from the same Archaic source. When symbology will be well understood, no intelligent man will meddle with the belief or unbelief of anyone.

The early Christian Fathers carried so far the principles of a double sense in Holy Writ, that they did not hesitate to declare that the Gospels were not truth according to the literal reading. "There are things contained therein," says Origen, "which, taken in their literal sense, are mere falsities and lies." St. Gregory, in the same vein, asserts that the whole divine letter is not only dead, but deadly. St. Anasthasius declares that, should we understand the sacred Scriptures according to the letter, we would fall into the most enormous blasphemies, and again we find: "God also hath made us able ministers of the New Testament, not of the letter, but of the spirit, for the letter killeth." St. Paul.

In the Kabala, secrecy is enforced in the most vehement terms: "Now," exclaims the author of the "Lesser Holy Assembly," "we have said that this is a symbol. Whosoever revealeth Arcana with fixed purpose of mind, he is not of the body of the Most Holy King. And whensoever his soul departeth the same adhereth not unto the body of the King, for it is not his place. Woe unto that man! woe unto himself! woe unto his Neschamah!"

CHAPTER V.

TYPOLOGY AND SYMBOLOGY.

"Theology is the box of Pandora; and if it is impossible to shut it, it is at least useful to inform men that this fatal box is open."— *Lord Bolingbroke.*

IT is claimed by occultists that they possess seven keys which unlock all the secret meanings contained in the sacred writings and ancient manuscripts the world at large possesses at present. However, several well-known writers have mastered typology and symbology, and demonstrated, most conclusively, the hidden meaning underlying the many-sided faces of the sphinxes of ancient times, without being initiated, or having penetrated the labyrinth of occultism. Says Madame Blavatsky, in her last work: "The complete records of the growth, development, social and even political life of the Lemurians have been preserved in the secret annals. Unfortunately, few are those who can read them, and those who could would still be unable to understand the language, unless acquainted with all the seven keys of its symbolism; for the comprehension of the occult doctrine is based on that of the seven sciences, which sciences find their expression in the seven different applications of the secret records to the exoteric texts. Thus, we have to deal with modes of thought on seven entirely different planes of ideality. Every text relates to, and has to be rendered from, one of the following standpoints:—

"1. The Realistic plane of thought.
"2. The Idealistic.
"3. The purely Divine or Spiritual.

"The other planes too far transcend the average consciousness, especially of the materialistic mind, to admit of their being even symbolized in terms of ordinary phraseology. There is no purely mythical element in any of the ancient religious texts, but the mode of thought in which they were originally written has to be found out, and closely adhered to, during the process of interpretation. For it is either symbolical (archaic mode of thought), emblematical (a later though very ancient mode of thought), parabolical (allegorical), hieroglyphical, or again logogrammatical, the most difficult mode of all, as every letter, as in the Chinese language, represents a whole word. Thus, almost every proper name, whether in the Vedas, the 'Book of the Dead,' or the Bible (to a degree) is composed of such logograms. No one who is not initiated into the mystery of the occult religious logography can presume to know what a name in any ancient fragment means, before he has mastered the meaning of every letter that composes it. How is it to be expected that the merely profane thinker, however great his erudition in orthodox symbolism, so to say, *i. e.*, in that symbolism which can never get out of the 'old grooves of Solar Myth and sexual worship,' shall penetrate into the arcane behind the veil. One who deals with the husk or shell of the dead letter, and devotes himself to the kaleidoscopic transformation of barren word symbols, can never expect to get beyond the vagaries of modern mythologists." No doubt there is a great deal of truth in the above statement. Yet two men, amongst others, have distinguished themselves greatly in the unriddling of the ancients' thoughts and ideas, as transmitted to us in their monuments and sacred writings. Those two men, Monsieur Gaston Maspero, successor to Mariette Bey, and Mr. Gerald Massey, have raised the veil which hid from multitudes the mysteries of ancient thoughts and personifications, and have unraveled them in their nakedness. They have interpreted mythology in its four phases: elemental, stellar, lunar, and solar, and traced back through typology and Onomatopcia (Massey), every glyph to its original source. As mankind developed the five senses we possess, now, gradually and imperceptibly, according to universal laws of progress and growth, it is easy to surmise that sight was the first sense with which men were endowed, as in Genesis, "Let light be." Therefore we can safely admit that Onomatopcia, or imitation of sounds, must have preceded speech. Says Gerald Massey: "There has been a mental evolution corresponding to the physical, and mythology retains the means of tracing the progress from the vague darkness through the stellar, lunar, and solar phases of thought into the later light of day. It is another mistake to imagine that primitive man began personifying, and, so to say, entifying the elements by conceiving the eidolon* of fire, wind, or water. Typology proves that he did not personify as his mode of representation. This process was mainly that of objective comparison. He represented one thing by another, the invisible force by a corresponding type of power. The process of representation was that which the logician terms in another application of the words, the substitution of similars. For instance, having no name for the moon, he saw that it was the eye of the dark, and called it the Cat, earlier lynx or lioness, whose golden eyes were luminous by night. This was the natural phase, but the image still served for typifying, when it was known that the moon was only a reflector of the solar light because the eye is a mirror. Hence the lunar cat-headed, or lioness-headed goddess became ·the eye of the sun. The primitive man did not animate the darkness or the water with any abstract spirit of destruction. But he realized the less definite swallower in the most definite form of the dragon, because he was compelled to think in things. He did not know how the earth gulped down the stars, or the water devoured the life, but he adopted the crocodile and hippopotamus as

---

*A duplicate or image of the thing defined.

forms most palpable. Earth was the visible cause of darkness, and therefore it was represented by the crocodile that swallowed the lights as they went down in the darkness. The serpent was that which darted death, so was the lightning. The hippopotamus was the power of the deluge broken out of bounds, the howling wind was the great ape in its wrath, the fire was the flaming yellow lion or the golden bird that soared aloft fearlessly in the flames of the sun.

This mode of expressing phenomena was the origin of the primordial types, which were continued as mythical, totemic, divine, and thus we are enabled to see that typology and mythology are twin from the birth, and one in their fundamental rootage. Primitive men were forced to typify in order that they might know by name these elemental energies and non-intellectual powers, even as they represented their own totems, and named themselves by means of the animals.

According to the laws of evolution, cognition of the unapparent power as cause of phenomena must have belonged to the latest perception, not the primary; and in its axiom of the present work that religious feeling originated in awe, and admiration of powers superior to those possessed by the human being, but that the nearest and most apparent were the earliest. The first so-called deities of primitive man may be called "weather god," and further on: "The most perplexing elements of mythology and language originate in the primary state of typology, the elementary and elemental." This passage, containing such invaluable hints to the student of symbology, cannot be, however, accepted in its entirety unless Darwinism should be recognized as absolute truth. Science tells us that the earth was a fiery ball, and under the cooling process solidified, but occultism goes still further back, assuring us that it was a shadow before it became a reality. Why should not man have followed the same laws of evolution? The cosmogonies of archaic races begin in the same manner, transmitting thus to us the universal idea of a beginning common to all nations, and embodied in a circle. It has been suggested that the cause of all, God, as the theologians want it, is a circle, the center of which is everywhere and the circumference nowhere. This wise definition is attributed to Laplace, who, it is contended, borrowed it from somebody else. Whoever gave it out first matters little, he certainly uttered the greatest and profoundest truth that mankind has ever received. Plato, in "Timæus," declares that the Deity geometrizes, and he describes the Creator as making the universe of a spherical form, the most like unto his own shape. We read in the " Secret Doctrine:" "The idea of representing the hidden Deity by the circumference of a circle, and the creative power, male and female, or the androgynous word by the diameter across it, is one of the oldest symbols. It is upon this conception that every great cosmogony was built. With the old Aryans, the Egyptians, and the Chaldeans, it was complete, as it embraced the idea of the eternal and immovable Divine Thought in its absoluteness, separated entirely from the incipient stage of the so-called creation; and comprised psychological and even spiritual evolution, and its mechanical work or cosmogonical construction."

Among the Quichés the same idea prevailed. In the mysteries instituted by Votan, the ballet of the Tapirs was an important feature in their celebration, and consisted of a dance executed by a certain number of venerable old men, who held a green palm in their hands, and turned in a solemn manner around a musician seated in the center of the circle they were describing. That the great mystic himself personated the musician, while he drew sonorous tunes from the Tunkul, is an illustration of the importance he attached to the symbolical circle. Votan's teachings were consistent with the pantheistic intuitions of archaic ages, they united harmoniously the visible with the invisible, the concealed Principle and Source of All, with its outward veil, the manifested universe. What a grand conception and how small the anthropomorphic god of the descendants of the Quiches appears, when compared with the glyph embodied in Votan's realistic circle!

The circle is the symbol of heaven, it is the perfected square, and the ancient philosophers always ascribed to it a mysterious and deep significance. It was essentially sacred to the initiates who saw in it a perpetual, never-ceasing evolution, "circling back in its incessant progress through æons of ages into its original status, Absolute Unity." It was the befitting emblem of life and immortality. Among the Hindus, the circle was represented by the Brahmanical golden egg, from which emerges the creative Deity. From the universal creed of the mundane egg, comes our custom of exchanging Easter eggs, in spring, the epoch of the renewal of life after the period of inaction, as during winter, though it must have originated after the more divine meaning of the circle had been forgotten, when it became the symbol of procreation, or rather begetting.

The egg was sacred to Isis; thus the Egyptian priests never ate any egg on that account, but it was, as we have just stated, after the ideal thought had degenerated. For the egg, as well as the circle and the wheel, was the glyph of life and immortality, though it was degraded afterwards into an emblem of the generative matrix. However, the Egyptians preserved its primitive significance in the winged globe and the winged Scarabeus. The name of the latter is suggestive of the occult idea attached to it. It means "to become," and refers to the rebirth of man as well as to his spiritual regeneration. It is the synthesis of human life in its successive becomings, through the various peregrinations and re-incarnations of progressive mankind.

Astronomically, we find that the planets belonging to our own solar system are identified with certain signs; the circle and the cross predominate because they are all crossers of the circle. Thus, the symbol of Mercury unites the moon, circle, and cross. Jupiter has a cross underneath a crescent. Mars has an oblique cross on the circle. Venus, a cross below the circle, Saturn, a sickle and a cross. In each case, the cross conveying the idea of the division of the circle into four angles of ninety degrees. The origin of the planetary signs is lost in the night of time; we can be assured of one thing, however, namely, that those who got them up knew mathematics and geometry to perfection, for the astronomical cross is the emblem of the circle of wisdom.

If we open the Bible, we are forcibly reminded of the mysterious and occult meaning of the circle in the passage describing the vision of the prophet Ezekiel, when "he beheld a whirlwind from which came out one wheel upon the earth whose work was as it were a wheel in the middle of a wheel— for the spirit of the living creature was in the wheels."

The mystic chain of the Masons, a reminiscence of ancient mysteries full of meaning, and of the highest import, is formed by making the circle with the hands of each person crossed. It derives all its significance from the cross and circle being figured at one and the same time, and as one and the same image, for the cross and the circle are so closely linked together that one cannot be interpreted without the other. For example, the circle having an inside cross is the symbol of fire and water, or the union of spirit and matter; though the first symbol in cosmogony is the circle, and the next one is the circle and diameter. In heraldry the square is but a broken or diminished circle, being the continuation of totem signs. Another illustration of the value and significance of the circle is found in the wedding-ring, "Lord send thy blessing upon this ring," the blessing being accompanied with the sign of the cross, emblem of the phallus, or multiplying ×, and this cross of four corners is the original source whereof the fourth digit was especially chosen to be the wearer of the wedding ring. It is the type of fertility of the circle fulfilled in the nine months of gestation, and it symbolizes children forever. Many ladies never take off their wedding-ring from the time it is put on the fourth finger at the altar, little thinking that it is a charm against miscarriage, and that when the custom originated, it conveyed the idea of reproduction.

The decimal system, as revived during the great French revolution, must have been known to the archaic races, since the astronomical and geometrical teachings of their philosophers are built upon the number ⊕ (10), which became later on a combination of the male and female principles. It was the foundation upon which the "Pyramid of Cheops" was built, that is, the digits combined with the nought.

We find it illustrated also in this figure ⊖ unity within zero, which was the emblem of the ever-existing principle, of the universe, and even of man. Such is the occult significance embodied in the "Master Masons grip," which is called also the "strong grip of the lion's paw," of the tribe of Judah, the joint number of the fingers of the two hands being synthesized in the mysterious number (10), one and a nought.

As stated repeatedly before, the "Absolute" could not be expressed by any word, therefore it was unutterable, and merely an idea which could not be expressed. "But," says Madame Blavatsky, "the symbol of its first comprehensible manifestation was the conception of a circle with its diameter line to carry at once a geometric, phallic, and astronomic idea, for the one takes its birth from the nought, or the circle, without which it could not be; and from one, or primal one, spring the nine digits, and geometrically all plane shapes." So in the Kabala this circle, with its diameter line, is the picture of the ten Sephiroth, or emanations, composing the Adam Kadmon, the archetypal man, the creative origin of all things. This idea of connecting the circle and its diameter line, that is, number 10, with the signification of the reproductive organs and the most holy place, was carried out constructively in the king's chamber or holy of holies of the great Pyramid, in the tabernacle of Moses, and in the holy of holies of the temple of Solomon. It is the picture of a double womb, for, in Hebrew, "he" is at the same time the number 5 and the symbol of the womb, and twice 5 is 10, or the phallic number. The double womb also shows the duality of the idea carried from the highest, spiritual, down to the lowest, or terrestrial, plane, and by the Jews limited to the latter. Finally, "Mandala" is in Sanscrit a circle or an orb, and it means also the ten divisions of the Rig-Veda.

The early Gnostics claimed that the Jehovah-Elohim of Genesis comprised a pleroma or circle consisting of Sophia, the genitrix, and her seven sons, whose names are as follows:—

1. Ialdabaoth, Lord God of the Fathers.
2. Iao—Javeh.
3. Sabaoth—Hosts.
4. Adoneus—Lord.
5. Eloeus—God.
6. Oreus—Light.
7. Astampheus—Crown.

This pleroma, or circle, is acknowledged by the Kabalists as constituting the totality of the Existent. It is sometimes termed Chivth.

Now, occultists, as well as Kabalists, reckon 3 kinds of lights: 1. The abstract and absolute light, which is darkness for us on this material plane. 2. The light of the Manifested emanating from the Unmanifested, better known under the name of Logos or Verbum, the Word. 3. The latter light reflected in the minor Logos or Elohim collectively, who in their turn shed it on the objective universe. The author of the "Source of Measures" says that the foundation of the Kabala and all its mystic books is made to rest upon the ten Sephiroth or Emanations, illustrated as follows: *i. e.*, they are contained in the circle and its diameter line, or the Pythagorean decade.

The Hebrew word "Zohar" means light, and from that sacred Jewish book we get the following statement: "When the first assumed the form of the crown or the first Sephira [the word Sephira or Sepher means to cipher], he caused nine splendid lights to emanate from it, which shining through it diffused a bright light in all directions, that is, these nine with his one [which was the origin, as above, of the nine] together made the ten, that is, ⊕ or ⊕ or the sacred ten (numbers or Sephiroth or Yod) and those numbers were the light." Just as in the gospel of St. John, God (Alhim, 31,415 to one) was that light (20,612 to 6,561) by which (light) all things were made.

Verse 1,152 of the Greater Holy Assembly (Kabala) expresses again the same profound idea: "We have learned that there were ten companions who entered into the sod or mysterious assembly, and that seven only came forth." This passage refers to the subjective and objective worlds synthesized in the circle and the line, of which 7 pertain to the manifested universe. Thus, for the Gnostics the visible and invisible cosmos was contained within; it could be expressed and described by the Pythagorean decade, or the digits of number 10. It could be studied from the universals of Plato and the inductive method of Aristotle. Such a system started from a divine comprehension of the unknown, from whom emanated the digits of the decade; plurality proceeding from unity was re-absorbed, and lost again in its original source, the circle. Thus, we will resume by saying that every cosmogony begins with a circle. It is followed by a point, a triangle, a cube, up to 9, which is synthesized by the circle accompanied by one line or 10, or again the sum and key of every mystery contained in either the objective or subjective universe. In occultism the circle is also synonymous of thought, and the diameter or line is the glyph for word, while the union of both is expressive of life. "And the earth was without form and void; and darkness was upon the face of the deep. And the Spirit of God moved upon the face of the waters." Genesis, chapter 1. In natural Genesis water is heaven, as the water above, and it is rendered by the circle, beginning of all cosmogony, even of the Jewish text describing the evolution of cosmos after its long rest in the eternal bosom of Ain-Soph, or Brahm.

TYPOLOGY AND SYMBOLOGY. 93

The tetragrammaton of the Western Kabalists is number 10. It is also personified by the circle, the pillar, the male and female Jehovah, and it is Pythagoras tetractis, because it is composed of 10 dots arranged triangularly in four rows.

The dance performed by King David was the circle dance, so was the circle described by the ancients in the sacred ballad of the Tapirs of Huehuetan, which was part of the mysteries instituted by Votan. In this case, as in the former, it was intended to denote the motion of the planets around the sun, thus conveying an astronomical imagery besides the occult interpretation, though Michal's taunt and the king's reply express the conception of a lower stage of symbolism.

It is claimed by many authors that the zodiac consisted, at first, only of ten signs, before the splitting up of Virgo—Scorpio. This hypothesis would allow occultism to connect the zodiacal divisions with the Kabalistic Sephiroth, who were nine, and ten when added to the Crown or Sephira, the emanative principle. From this theory was derived the Pythagorean Decade. It was composed of three trinities with the "One Source of All;" it represents the whole cosmos, and was written upon the heavens in indelible letters, as the primitive ten signs of the zodiac, corresponding to the Demiurgus and his nine assistants.

CHAPTER VI.
NUMBER 3 AND NUMBER 7.

"Let no man judge you for your observance of the seventh day and the day of the new moon, which are a shadow of things to come."—*St. Paul.*

NUMBER 3 AND NUMBER 7.

As stated before, the first gods were all weather gods, or, rather, personifications of air or ether. We find the original ideal symbolized in Brahma, Zeus, Hurukan, Gucumatz, Quetzalcohualt, and even in the "Spirit of God," brooding over the waters in the initial chapter of Genesis. "As Kasa is the becoming visible or apparent, Akasa is the invisible or unapparent. But in this elemental stage, the unapparent is not god, it is only atmospherical. Ether is represented by the cone as the fifth sign in the diagram, in which the square signifies earth, the circle, water (heaven as the water above), the pyramid or triangle, fire, the crescent, air, and the cone, ether, which, as fifth, was once the quintessence of the elements. The full number of these is seven in India, Egypt, Britain and other countries. The seven elements from which came the seven spirits of mythology are identified by the British Barddas as earth, water, fire, air, ether, or vapor, blossom (the seminal principle), and the wind of purpose (or the ghost). A sixth element was known among the Hindus as Bala-rama, the representation of masculine virility. Bala denotes force considered as a sixth form or mode of manifestation. It is the innate strength of the male, the semen virile. This is the sixth element, the fructifying principle of the Druids named blossom. The seventh was the soul and summit of the rest. Elementary types or gods were founded on the elements, and they are symbols of the elements which were typified."—*Typology*. There are seven properties in nature,—matter, cohesion, fluxion, coagulation, accumulation, station, and division. But it is old Egypt that affords us a test-type for the unity of origin in mythology as portrayed in the Great Mother, the boundless, limitless, primordial chaos, the genitrix of all, and her seven sons.

The celebrated writer and occultist Ehphas Levi (l'abbé Louis Constant) said that the Sepher Jezirah, the Zohar and the Apocalypse of St. John, are the masterpieces of the occult sciences. He might have added, so far as the Jewish Scriptures are concerned, for there are deeper works extant, though it must be admitted that the works just mentioned above contain far greater significance than words, and that while in numbers they are exact, the expressions used throughout are poetical. But to be able to appreciate their true merit, the student has to be conversant with the meaning of the terms and symbols in which the ideas are rendered. To master those works he will have to thoroughly understand the value in all their different aspects of the names of gods, angels, patriarchs, etc., as given in the Jewish Bible, besides their mathematical or geometrical value, and their relations to objective universe.

Thus, the Sacred Books of the ancients, the Vedas, the Popol-Vuh, the Zend-Avesta, the Book of the Dead, the Chaldean Tablets, Hesiod's Theogony, and others, at which our learned men were either sneering, or were admiring their simplicity, become the many-sided sphinxes of archaic ages. Many ponder over their ambiguous texts, but few are the Œdipuses who solve the riddle!

It is generally admitted that number 3 is the number *par excellence*. It is the male number, and as the triangle $\triangle$ is the symbol for light, and the emblem of $\triangle$ the Concealed One. It is the first of the odd numbers, and it is also the first of the geometrical figures. Numberless combinations can be applied to it, and none has rendered them more thoroughly than Ragon in his "Cours interpretatif des Initiations," that is, so far as the exoteric significance is concerned. In the Hindu symbolism of numerals the esoteric interpretation is expounded for the benefit of those who can fathom it. The occult properties of the three equal lines or sides of the triangle inspired Ragon with the true basis of his studies on the subject, and also with the idea of establishing his famous society of the "Trinosophists," or " Fellows who study three sciences," which is a great improvement upon the ordinary way of conferring Masonic degrees. The first line of the triangle offered to the apprentice for study, says the founder, is the mineral kingdom, symbolized by Tubal Cain. The second side on which the " companion " has to meditate is the vegetable kingdom, represented by Shibboleth. In this kingdom begins the generation of bones. This is why the letter " G " is unfolded radiant before the eyes of the adept. The third side is left to the Master Mason, who has to complete his education by the study of the animal kingdom. It is symbolized by Maoben (sun of putrefaction).

With the Pythagoreans the origin of differentiation, of contrasts and discord, in fact, the beginning of matter, and therefore of evil, was all traceable to the binary; hence even numbers were considered the sum total of all that is unlucky and devilish. Number one alone was the synthesis of harmony, and of all that is good, because no discord can exist where there is only one.  But the ternary is, verily, the mysterious number *par excellence*. It is essentially spiritual, though under one of its phases it becomes the emblem of the principle underlying the formation of physical, or animal, bodies.

The Kabala identifies the primordial trinity with the three true witnesses who testify to the nature of the Infinite One; they are the three upper Sephiroth, as in verse 1,152 of the Greater Holy Assembly: "We have learned that there were ten companions who entered into the sod (Mystery) and that only seven came forth." Leo de Modena, an orthodox Jew, wondered at the possibility of forgiving those who printed the Kabalistic works, as the doctrine of the triad contained in them had led many Jews to abandon the faith of their fathers, and become Christians. What is more deplorable still, is that what is called the civilized world is groaning under the iron yoke of theology founded upon the empty shadows of the same great truths. The sooner symbolism will be taught publicly, the better for the Christian nations.

Three distinct representations of the universe, under three different aspects, become impressed upon our mind by the leading philosophical systems: (1) The pre-existing evolving from the ever-existing, (2) and the phenomenal world, the manifested universe, (3) which is only the shadow and reflection of its prototype, and, consequently, a mere illusion, though it seems real enough to those who are in it. Such is the origin of the mythical trinity, whose source is to be found in the central eternal germ of the Brahminical Egg, or the unity.

Among the ancient relics of old Egypt we find the infant Horus seated in the decans of the Ram, holding the whip of rule in his left hand and the starry triangle in his right, and Proclus employing the same imagery as a figure of speech when he says, "The celestial triangle is connective of all generation, being proximate to the Ram." But the typological trinity was: mother, son, and pubescent male. The mother, the genitrix, was chaos, the boundless space, the pre-existing universe; her child was the manifested world, and the two were evolved from the ever-existing. Such was the archaic ideal, the first conception of the mythical trinity. We read in the Litany of Ra: "Thou commandest the Osirified deceased to be like Khuti, the brilliant 'Triangle,' which appears in the shining place." Thus (typology) "the dead rose on the horizon of the resurrection," like the sun in the sign of the vernal equinox when that was the ram in the shape of the triangle, as an image of the trinity in unity. The triple Horus was the threefold sun, which was unified once a year, at the time and at the place of the spring equinox. There is a form of him as the child crowned with a triple crown of reed, and called the "Lord of the world." It was he who divided the upper from the lower heaven, as stated in Ephesians 14: "For he is our peace who hath made both one and hath broken the middle wall of partition between us." From the same idea originated the dividing wall of the second court of the temple of Jerusalem. Thus the human triad was copied from the celestial, as the visible universe is an image of its invisible pattern.

Among the Quichés we find again the same thought, as illustrated in Hurakan, or Voice of Thunder, Lightning, and Thunder-bolt, the triad contained in the "Heart of Heaven," which sprung out of that primitive religious sentiment which clothed the uncomprehended powers of nature with the attributes of divinity.

The mystery contained in the ancient wisdom has to be unfolded in numbers rather than in geometrical figures or letters, though the figure Iao is not only indicated by the triangle, but also by the mystic AUM of the Hindus, and the IAO of the Jews. From Plutarch we learn that the Egyptians held the divine nature to consist of three, and this trinity was typified by the triangle, the base thereof being feminine, the perpendicular masculine, and the subtense the product of both. They also considered Osiris as the first cause, or the sun; Isis, as the recipient, or the moon, and Horus, as the child, or effect. In Lucian's auction there is a Pythagorean dialogue in which the great philosopher asks, "How do you reckon?" It is answered: "One, two, three, four." Then says the wise Greek, "Do you not see that in what you conceive four, there are ten—a perfect triangle and our oath?" In the

Hebrew sheba, the oath, is identical with number 7, and taking an oath was synonymous with "to seven," though the Greek oath was, "By three am I overthrown."

In the Hebraic secret works the last three Sephiroth constitute the natural world, or nature in its essence, and in its active principle; they embody the symbolism of the generative element of all that is. In the three tetragrammatic forms, which give twelve letters, is found the trinity of the tetragram, the trinity in unity, proceeding from the concealed unity and expressed in the thirteen divisions of the Beard of Macroprosopus, or the Kabalistical glyph synthesizing unity.

In Rome were, we may say, amalgamated the versions of the Egyptian, Hebrew, Greek, and Mithraic primitive myths, and re-issued as dogmas of a new religion. The mother, the archaic genitrix of the Great Bear, or of chaos, and her son holding the foremost position until about the thirteenth century of our era, when God the Father succeeded in displacing the Virgin of the world, but without despoiling her of her popularity; for she came from herself to occupy a position belonging to her by right, and her son was born but not begotten. Thus, in the Greek iconography, to the triangle of Horus, the nimbus or glory of the god is added; and the Holy Ghost of the middle age also wears the triangular aureole. In a fresco of the Cathedral of Auxerre, the god holds a book in his left hand,

and with his right hand he makes the sign of the Trinity in the orthodox way of the Catholic Church, the thumb and two forefingers being uplifted, and the other two closed. Such is the origin of the papal blessing bestowed upon the people by the bishops of the Romish Church, and the meaning of the ring they wear on their middle finger is part of the mystery: it is the circle which contains the three, or Trinity. Though the triangle, the emblem of the concealed One, has become the symbol of God the Father among Christians, Mary, the Genitrix, the Great Mother, the exalted Sophia of the Gnostics, has maintained her prominent position with her child Horus, or the Messiah. The primitive conception of the Trinity was also perpetuated by the ancients in the third sign of the zodiac, Gemini, the embodiment of the dual deity as rendered by the Kabalists; Sephira, Adam Kadmon; and by the Hindus as the Androgyne Brahma, the one who becomes two.

The two triangles are generally called Solomon's seal, and as six they denote the union of the two sexes, but if we combine the triangle with the quaternary or light and life, we have the septenary man the "Heavenly Man," or Microprosopus, who is also called the manifested Logos.

Among the ancients, number 7, or the triangle in

the square, or again gles, was a symbol Sevekh was synonythe Hebrew deity of the seven letters. and India were cele- 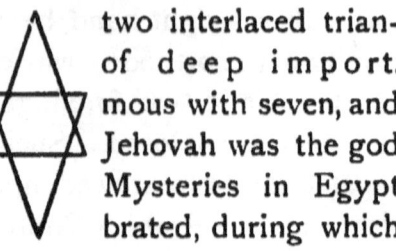 two interlaced triangles of deep import. mous with seven, and Jehovah was the god Mysteries in Egypt brated, during which the utterance of the seven vowels was an important feature. The Greek Zeus, the father of all living, had his name beginning with a double seven, thus Z, and the initial letter for "I live" in the Greek language is a Z or double seven. One need not wonder then because seven should have been adopted as the synthesis of the union of terrestrial man with his celestial prototype; under this aspect it becomes the emblem of eternal life. Moreover, Zeus means ether, and the Aryan Dyaus, which is also the Latin Deus, can be rendered by day or light, while the German Gott and the English God are both derived from the Hebrew yod, the phallic hook.

The seven vowels as printed by Bunsen are: A, E, E, I, O, O, U; they are contained potentially in the A, I, U, of the Egyptians and Copts, and expressed by the words to come and to go, and are an emblem of duality. The I, U, or A, of the beginning and O of the end mean also, was, it, and to be. Thus, the personified duad, linked with the triad, became a combination of a threefold one with a sevenfold manifestation, as we find it illustrated in the seven Sephiroth, seven Rishis, seven spirits or seven breaths, etc.

Number 7 was prominent in astronomy and most sacred to the Jews from antiquity on account of its relation to the moon, our satellite. Their sabbath or seventh day originated from the fourfold number 7 being contained in the twenty-eight days of the lunar month; each septenary portion thereof being typified by one-quarter of the moon: "And on the seventh day Elohim ended his work which he had made; and he rested on the seventh day from all his work which he had made. And Elohim blessed the seventh day and sanctified it, because that in it he had rested from all his work which Elohim created and made." Genesis, chapter II. This passage, frequently quoted as authority for keeping the Sabbath, or seventh day, does not refer here to days but cycles of obscuration or repose, and of manifestation or activity. Hence, the creator of the Bible is not the universal unless blended with Ain-Soph, called also Microprosopus, or Non-Being, but he is one of the septenaries of the universal septenate. The Kabala teaches that the words, " Fiat Lux" (Genesis, chapter I), refer to the formation and evolution of the Sephiroth, and not to light as opposed to darkness. Rabbi Simeon says: "O companions, companions, man as an emanation was both man and woman, Adam Kadmon verily, and this is the sense of the words, 'Let there be light and it was light.' And this is the twofold man (Zohar)." In its unity, the light of the unmanifested Logos is the primordial light, the highest or seventh principle emphasized by the central point of the interlaced triangles; but as the collective Logos, or lower Sephiroth, it is seven. The latter is also symbolized by the hexagon or six limbs of the Microprosopus, the lesser face, with Malkuth, the "bride" of the Christian Kabalists, as the seventh (or our earth). Therefore the first triangle of the Pythagorean triad corresponds to the Tetragrammaton which is at the head of the seven lower Sephiroth, or collective Logos. The Zohar explains that the primordial elements, the trinity of fire, air and water, △ the four cardinal points, ☐ and all the voices of nature form collectively the "Word," the "Voice of the Will," or the "Logos." Hence it is said that the Tetragrammaton is the three made four, and the four made three, and that it is represented on this earth by his seven companions or eyes,—the "seven eyes of the Lord."

The origin and significance of numbers is closely linked with the seven stars of Ursa Major. Seven was not only a perfect number, but also a lucky number, conveying an idea of abundance, as its Egyptian name, Hept, meant plenty. It was also the image of the revolution of time, for Pythagoras tells us that the two Bears were the two hands of the Great Mother, whose names, Kheb and Teb, meant the hand and the finger, as she supplied the pointer hand to the celestial horologe of time.

They were also dual in this sense that they typified the Mother or She-bear, and her son, or progeny. The Great Bear was also identical with the genitrix Rhea, consort of Kronus, and with the earlier personification of the same glyph under the name of Typhon and Sevekh, her son. These two were Kep the mother, and Kheb the child, or the seven companions. Kep means the hand, and ti is two or twin, and Kepti is both hands, or number 7. In this case the left or lower hand is feminine, and the right, or upper one, is masculine.

Wherever and whenever we find number 7 mentioned in the sacred ancient books, we may rely upon a double sense being attached to the sentence. Hence, when we read in the Bible that Moses married one of the seven daughters of his father-in-law Jethro, and we become aware that her name, Zipphorah, reads the "shining one," we may be assured that no real marriage in the sense we attach to the word took place, but that Moses was initiated by Jethro into the mysteries of occult sciences, and that solely on that account he was the son of his initiator. It is a phraseology commonly employed between members of the same brotherhood. We may also mention that the well by which Moses sat down and rested in his flight, symbolized a well of knowledge. Astronomically and geologically, number 7 is also connected with the constellation of the Pleiades, and historically with the Grecian myth relating to the seven daughters of Atlas, who were

Maia, Electra, Taygeta, Asterope, Merope, Alcyone, and Celæno. They are called the Atlantides, because they represent the seven sub-races of the lost continent, so frequently referred to by the Egyptians, the Quichés, and the Mayas. After the submersion of the lands occupied by the races they personify they were assigned a place in the heavens. Occultism attributes to them an influence of high import, asserting that they rule the destinies of nations according to the laws of cause and effect, better known now under the name of Karmic law. It is even hinted that we are now paying the iniquities committed by us while imprisoned in Titanic bodies, during the fourth race period; for the continents of Lemuria and Atlantis are combined and personified in the allegory of Atlas.

In natural genesis, as well as in esotericism, both constellations of the Great Bear and the Pleiades hold a foremost position, the former as the genitrix, the great Mother and her seven sons, identical with the seven Rishis, seven planetary spirits, seven Sephiroth, seven Amshaspands, seven companions, seven Kabiri, seven principles of man, seven cosmic principles, etc., symbolizes the evolving principle of the cosmic forces, and is also identical with the lower Sephiroth; while the Pleiades are the sidereal septenate, born from the first manifested side of the upper triangle, also known as the concealed $\triangle$ This manifested side is Taurus the symbol of one, the first letter of the

Hebrew alphabet, which is Aleph, the Phœnician and Hebrew calf. Here we find the motive that induced the Jews to worship the calf in the desert. It was the emblem of duality, the calf being of either sex.

The Pleiades are the central group of the system of sidereal symbology in esotericism, and in astronomy they are the central point around which our universe revolves. The center star, Alcyone, is considered as the nucleus into which are focussed all the forces which are working incessantly under the cosmic laws of our present Manvantara. Therefore, in astronomical symbolism, the Pleiades, or the circle with the starry cross on its face, hold the most prominent place, and in occultism they are attributed a marked influence upon our destinies. Though the star Alcyone is a powerful sun, twelve thousand times superior to our yellow sun in volume and brilliancy, yet with the naked eye it seems unimportant and ordinary, and we must confess that the ancients must have been endowed with the cyclopean eye, or must have possessed telescopes in order to recognize and appreciate the important part assumed by the central star of the constellation Pleiades.

We are told by occultists that man is a septenary being, endowed with seven principles, and that every globe (our earth included) belongs to a septenary chain of worlds, of which only one is visible, and that every one of them is, was, or will be, man-bearing, though they may not be gotten up upon the pattern of our present human races, for the law of nature is uniformity in diversity.

The seven cosmic principles are: Earth or matter, vivifying universal spirit, astral or cosmic atmosphere, cosmic will, astral light or universal ilusion, universal mind, and latent spirit.

The seven principles in man are: The body, the life-principle, the astral body, the animal soul or will, the human soul or mind, the spiritual soul, and the Divine Spirit. Each one of those principles represents a plane of consciousness, and is analogous to the state and sense corresponding to it. We have now five senses, we are in the fifth Root-race, and we are just developing the human soul, or mind. We have still to acquire two more senses, and when we possess seven senses we will have reached the goal of human attainment on this earth. Occultists claim, likewise, that until the highest planetary spirits evolve a higher stage of perfection, which will allow them to assimilate themselves to the essence of worlds lying beyond our own solar system, they will remain in ignorance of a plane of consciousness which is now forbidden ground on account of the law of analogy.

In the Chaldean tablets there is a description of the seven kings of Edom, who were sexless. Now it is claimed that Esau was their father, and that they personify the attempts at producing a perfect physical man, the pre-Adamic races referred to in the Quiché and Toltec manuscripts. They are left out of calculation in Genesis because they impersonate the shadowy seven primordial sub-races, and refer to the first seven kings of Edom; but Esau, Jacob's son, is typifying the race which stands for them between the fourth and the fifth.

In the Grecian allegory of Niobe, the mother of seven sons and seven daughters, we find again a myth perpetuating the history of continents, races, and climatic changes. Niobe is the daughter of one of the Pleiades or Atlantides, and consequently a granddaughter of Atlas, and as such she typifies the last generations of the doomed continent. We say doomed, because it is claimed by occultists that the sons of Will and Yoga, of the third race, became indignant at the vices of the Atlanteans, and that Niobe's children were annihilated by Latona's children Apollo and Diana, who, as personifications of the sun and the moon, are intended to convey the idea of the geological and climatic changes due to the influence they exercise upon the earth's axis.

The same version of the myth of the Hyades, sisters of the Pleiades, can be obtained if following closely the run of rounds, root-races and sub-races.

Apollo is the sun, he is the god of the seers and the patron of the mysterious number 7, for he was born on the 7th of the month, and the swans of Myorica celebrated that event by swimming seven times around Delos. The swan is a symbol of duality typifying either air and water, or fire and water, if applied to elements, but it is also an emblem of the union of spirit with matter. Astronomically Apollo is given seven chords to his lyre, he is represented with the circle of the seven rays of the sun, and his name is linked with the seven forces of nature.

Jehovah, the Who? of the Kabala, the deity of the seven vowels, became, under the compound name of Iao-Sabaoth, the god of the seven planets. Each planet corresponded to one of the seven vowels and to one of the seven notes of the scale. Moreover, each day of the week was dedicated to one of the seven vowels, and to one of the planets. In the seven notes of the scale, and the orbit lines of the planet, the distribution was as follows:—

Ut or Do, Mercury; Re, Venus; Mi, Sun; Fa, Mars; Sol, Jupiter; La, Saturn, in making the music of the Spheres. Dion Casio declares that the names given to the days of the week had for an object to express, under a philosophical form, the occult relations existing between the divisions of time, and the order of the stars that regulated its course, uniting besides under the same mathematical conception the harmonies of the celestial movements with the harmonious intervals of musical tones. Such is the origin of the names given by the archaic races to the days of the week. The Germans, however, preferred the names of their own gods to those of the planetary deities.

In Revelation the repetition of number 7 occurs constantly. There are seven churches, the book is sealed with seven seals. "And when he had opened the seventh seal, there was silence in heaven about the space of half an hour. And I saw the seven angels which stood before God, and to them were given seven trumpets." Chapter 8. And again in chapter 11: "And the seventh angel sounded; and there were great voices in heaven saying, The kingdoms of the world are become the kingdoms of our Lord, and of his Christ, and he shall reign forever and ever. In chapter 13 a beast riseth out of the sea with seven heads and ten horns, to whom the dragon giveth his power.

Chapter 15 describes the seven angels with the seven last plagues and the seven vials full of the wrath of God. Why are Christians so blind as not to see that the occult symbolism underlying the book of Revelation, is a science which they have to master before they can pretend to understand it?

The deep occult meaning which underlies the zodiacal sign of Virgo-Scorpio is well known among mystics. All the Kabalists and Hermetists call the Astral Light the "heavenly or celestial Virgin." Therefore Virgo, as the sixth sign of the zodiacal divisions, is befittingly represented by the two triangles; the point or crown, as the unity, is the seventh because there are seven principles diffused in every unity.

CHAPTER VII.

THE DRAGON, THE SERPENT, AND THE CROSS.

"The monogram, or symbol of the God Saturn, was the sign of the cross, together with a ram's horn in imitation of the Lamb of God."—*Rev. Robert Taylor.*

As stated before, St. John's Revelation is one of the masterpieces of occult science, and we cannot begin our glossary on the dragon with more fitting words than those of St. John himself: "And there appeared a great wonder in heaven, a woman clothed with the sun, and the moon under her feet, and upon her head a crown of twelve stars. And she being with child, cried, travailing in birth, and pained to be delivered.

"And there appeared another wonder in heaven; and behold, a great red dragon, having seven heads and ten horns, and seven crowns upon his head.

"And his tail drew the third part of the stars of heaven, and did cast them to the earth, and the dragon stood before the woman which was ready to be delivered, for to devour her child as soon as it was born. And she brought forth a man-child, who was to rule all nations with a rod of iron; and her child was caught up unto God and to his throne.

"And the woman fled into the wilderness, where she hath a place prepared of God, that they should feed her there a thousand two hundred and threescore days.

"And there was war in heaven; Michael and his angels fought against the dragon; and the dragon fought and his angels,

"And prevailed not; neither was their place found any more in heaven."

The myth referred to in this passage by St. John was so universal that it is identically related in the Grecian Theogony, and has survived in the Roman Catholic cult in the person of the Virgin Mary.

In the "Secret Doctrine" we find an able interpretation of this legend. "So occult and mystic is one of the aspects of Latona that she is made to re-appear even in Revelation as the woman clothed with the sun (Apollo) and the moon (Diana) under her feet, who, being with child, cries, travailing in birth, pained to be delivered. A great red dragon stands before the woman ready to devour the child. She brings forth the man-child who was to rule all nations with a rod of iron, and who was caught unto the throne of God (the sun). The woman fled to the wilderness, still pursued by the dragon, who flies again, and casts out of his mouth water as a flood, when the earth helped the woman and swallowed the flood, and the dragon went to make war with the remnant of her seed who keep the commandment of God." Anyone who reads the allegory of Latona pursued by the typhon sent by Juno to devour her baby, will recognize the identity of the two versions. The baby is Apollo, the sun; for the man-child who was to rule all nations with an iron rod of revelation is surely not the meek Son of God Jesus, but the physical sun who rules all nations, the dragon being the north pole gradually chasing the early Lemurians from the lands which became more and more hyperborean and unfit to be inhabited by those who were fast developing into physical men, for they had now to deal with climatic variations. The dragon will not allow Latona to bring forth, the sun to appear. She is driven from heaven, and finds no place where she can bring forth, until Neptune (the ocean), moved with pity, makes immovable the floating isle of Delos, the nymph Asteria (hitherto hiding from Jupiter under the waves of the ocean), on which Latona finds refuge, and where the bright god Apollo is born; the god no sooner appears than he kills Python, the cold and frost of the Arctic regions in whose deadly coils all life becomes extinct. In other words, Latona-Lemuria is transformed into Niobe-Atlantis, over which her son Apollo, or the sun, reigns with an iron rod truly, since Herodotus makes the Atlantes curse his too great heat. Latona became a powerful goddess, and her cult has been always growing, every one of her attributes having been revived by the Popish Church, her son, the sun, being the great solar god of antiquity, and of Christendom.

The war in heaven is essentially an astronomical myth which was preserved by the archaic races, and was transmitted to posterity in the legends of the war of the Titans against the gods in Hesiod; in the war of the Asuras against the Devas, and in the Central American Quinamés against the gods. It has been proven that at the time of the war in heaven, all the planets, except Saturn, were in conjunction, and, according to Hesiod and Moses, Saturn, or the moon-god, prevailed. Undoubtedly the whole passage formerly quoted has been gotten up to perpetuate the remembrance of terrible revolutions and cataclysms in the heavens and on earth; because the two poles anciently denoted a good and a bad dragon, the former typifying the north pole, or heaven of the hyperboreans, and the latter the south pole, abode of the cosmic elementals.

All the archaic races reverenced the symbol of the dragon; hence we encounter it in every mythology. The oldest nation in our present humanity is the Chinese, and among her people we find the emblem of the dragon surviving in spite of changes of dynasties, and still flying in high colors on the national standard. The emperor's throne is the dragon's seat, and his dresses of state are embroidered with the likeness of the dragon. The aphorisms in the oldest Chinese books point plainly to an occult significance, for they extol the yellow dragon as the chief of all, and as a being endowed with unfathomable wisdom and virtue on account of his living alone, which means that he is an ascetic. He wanders in the heavens wherever he pleases, fulfilling the decree, or Karma; he is an embodiment of the Christian Providence in that respect, portraying also perfection and wisdom. Sut-Typhon, the Egyptian dragon, was of a red complexion like the dragon of Revelation, the same hue being retained for the giants, and in the Beard of Thunder, who was killed by Jack the giant killer. The word "Tenny" in English heraldry means the dragon's head.

The dragon is also associated with the early legend of the serpent of Paradise, who wished to impart knowledge to the first pair, for it is said that he taught Fohi how the sexes were divided. It is for the same reason that the Ophites held the serpent in such high esteem. They claimed that the first pair were initiated into the mysteries by the dragon, who taught them that which divided the sexes. Therefore the dragon was essentially a mystic symbol linked with the primeval glyphs, for his soul resided in the Great Bear, the words soul and star being synonymous in the Egyptian language.

It is held by symbologists that primitively the two constellations of the Great Bear and Little Bear were only one, or the mother and her progeny, her seven sons. The crocodile or dragon is one type in Egyptian, and sevekh means 7. This assertion is sustained by the astronomer Proctor, who claims that the Lesser Bear was in ancient times a portion of the dragon; and his opinion is corroborated by the explanation of the myth of the dragon, or Egyptian crocodile. To the same symbol we can trace back the seven crowns of Revelation, who were the seven-headed dragon of the pole. "The pole of the world is called the soul of Rhea (Typhon) by the Pythagoreans," exclaims Proclus.

"There is a polar dragon whose coilings round and round on itself when A-Draconis was a pole-star, were made at the pivotal center of motion in the planisphere, and with the Lesser Bear for its seven heads we can identify the seven-headed dragon of the Mythos."—*Natural Genesis.*

The dragon as a glyph preceded the serpent as an emblem of the geological phase preceding the formation of our earth, *i. e.*, before it was the fit abode of human races. It is linked with a creation which was sunk below the waters. Therefore it was not accidentally that the northern shaft of the pyramid of Gizeh was built like a huge telescopic tube focussing the star A-Draconis, which has been the pole-star, and is on its way back to the polar center of starry motion.

Another type of the Typhonian genitrix, or great Bear, is the unicorn; because horn is an emblem of duration, and beasts prevail on account of their power of resistance. The Ritual mentions the horn and the beak. When in the ascendant, Venus is said to be on the horn, and the red dragon of Revelation had ten horns. The national arms of England contain a copy of Typhon personifying the unicorn and the lion. Philo says that in the symbol of the coiled-up snake, the eye in the center had to be visible inside of the circle. In the emblem of the seven-headed dragon turning round on its inner eye, the interpretation is identical, the polar star, or dragon's eye, being the pivot of heavenly revolutions. The tree with the seven branches, of the Mithra cult, is also surrounded with the sun, moon, and seven stars, and a male and a female. It signifies the birthplace of the beginning, around which the seven-headed dragon, Typhon, or crocodile, is continually revolving. Hesiod describes the terrible dragon that watches the all golden apples lying in a cavern of the dark earth, at its furthest extremity. Prometheus, the divine benefactor of rising humanity, persuaded Hercules to send Atlas for the coveted fruit while he should assume provisionally the place of supporter of the heavens. This legend, which reveals an interesting part of the history of our globe, ends with the hero carrying the golden apples to the north, because it was the center of heaven and the seat of the good dragon.

Astronomically, the dragon of the north pole, or the Great Bear, personified one revolution, year, annus, or cycle, and was an intelligencer to men, the indicator of seasons, solstices, and equinoxes. But when men became aware that there was a change taking place, that A-Draconis was losing its place, then it became the bad dragon. The sign was rejected as false. Thus there were two dragons, one typifying good, and its opponent representing evil. Under this latter aspect it is Apophis, the monster of theology, or Kakodemon, the black one. He is the eternal adversary of Agathodemon, the good serpent.

The dragon was universally connected with number 7 in India, as the seven-headed Sesha; in Egypt, as the crocodile-dragon sevekh, or seven, and the seven-headed dragon of Akkad, because it indicated the end of a cycle, or period. Linked with an idea of flood, deluge, dispersion, or cataclysm, it typifies the conclusion of an age contemporaneous with the stellar imagery, and the dawn of a new era; the cast-out dragon gave place to the solar god. Apollo, the brilliant son of Latona, kills Python, the dragon, and takes his place as the inspirer of the oracles; hence light supersedes darkness.

"And I beheld another beast coming up out of the earth, and he had two horns like a lamb, and he spake as a dragon. And he exerciseth all the power of the first beast before him, and causeth the earth and them which dwell therein to worship the first beast, whose deadly wound was healed." Now, the beast with the two horns typifies the lamb, or the epoch when the sun entered the sign of the Ram, and dethroned the old dragon, by taking its place. Under this aspect, Typhon is transformed into the solar crocodile, who lays sixty eggs, is sixty days in hatching them, and lives sixty years. Thus was transmitted to posterity the first measure adopted by Egyptian astronomers. "Here is wisdom. Let him that hath understanding count the number of the beast; for it is the number of a man, and his number is six hundred threescore and six." As stated formerly, the wisdom contained in occult works is frequently rendered in numbers. Thus, in this instance the dawn of the new era inaugurated by the entrance of the sun into the Ram is typified by the four corners, and the Nadir and Zenith, or number 6. In the Egyptian symbology it combines the planetary and solar character in the personification of Saturn and Ra, or the sun. Blended together it leaves only six planets, a reduction of one, from the wounded cast-out beast or dragon, who lost one of its heads.

The three letters S. S. S. accompany the seven-rayed solar dragon, and the three S's are generally read as 666. Vishnu, in his solar character, is related to number 6 as the type of the six directions of space. The Abrasax was the six-sided cube figure of the solar foundation, and Sut, the son of

Typhon, is also number 6, because his birthplace was in the south, hence his name, Su or S. S. S. There is a tradition pointing to the fact that the Egyptian priests told Herodotus that the sun did not always rise in the north, therefore a reminiscence of its former birthplace, the south, was treasured as sacred, and the beast of Revelation being also identified with 666, or S. S. S., which is related with the name of a man as Pharaoh, or number 43, we may safely conclude that the second beast with the two horns was identical with the beginning of a new cycle inaugurated by the sun entering a new sign, the sign of the Ram; it was the signal of a final planetary stage symbolized by Saturn, who is also represented with a ram's horn, or a crescent, combining the symbol of the moon and the lamb. Such is the origin of the Jewish god Jehovah, the moon-god, and the Christian Lamb, or Son of God, Jesus Christ, sprung from the same source.

Elemental, stellar, lunar, solar, each phase has to develop from the one preceding it. The great dragon combines the four elements of the abyss, and is in its turn dethroned by the Lunar-Mythos, represented by the female slayer of the dragon, who becomes the female Jehovah of the Jews. The latter is the mirror, or reflector, of the sun. Hence, the woman in the Ritual boasts that she made the "eye of Horus" when it was not forthcoming at the fifteenth day of the month. Such is the origin of the "eye" as a symbol of deity. A woman standing on a globe, in the act of bruising the head of the serpent, is frequently seen in the Roman Catholic Church; it is a perfect counterpart of the woman of the planisphere. It is on Christmas-day, when Jesus Christ, Krishna, Buddha, Apollo, Osiris, or any of the sun-gods, are born that the constellation Virgo arises on the horizon holding the new babe in her arms, and trodding underfoot the serpent. That woman was Isis with her child Horus in Egypt; it is now Mary with the infant Jesus among the Christians. It is also the woman of Revelation.

Typhon, the mythical dragon, combined the abyss, or source of all things, in itself; it was emblematically rendered by the hole of the snake, and also by the egg that emanated from the mouth of the serpent, because it typified a circle, revolution, or age. Such is the origin of our Easter eggs.

We have explained in a former chapter the part played by the serpent in the biblical fall. Let us only add that some of the Rabbis relate that the old serpent having shed his own skin presently after the fall of man, Elohim made a garment of it to clothe Adam and Eve. This process of re-clothing the Adam of the fall is evidently a myth, embodying the first initiation of material men into the deep mysteries of renovation and spiritual re-birth; for the sloughing snake was essentially an emblem of transformation. Magnificent ruins attest to the present day the grandeur of the glyph embodied in the serpent, and the acknowledged dominion of its secret mysteries. It was venerated by the ancients as a symbol of eternity, of re-birth, of immortality, of wisdom. None has impressed the mysterious attributes of the serpent more strongly than Votan, the great Quiché legislator, who was, he declares, the son of a serpent, and yet a serpent himself. In such capacity he entered a subterranean passage that ran to the roots of heaven, which was only the hole of a snake. This was a term used by initiates synonymous with circle of necessity, and inevitable circle. It was also the circle of transformation when referring to the human races. Proclus states that in the most holy mysteries the neophytes were divested of their garments to participate in a divine nature. The new robe was the garment of salvation; it was accounted sacred, and held in the greatest esteem by the adepts, who associated their new raiment with their spiritual and divine re-birth. As initiates they were called "serpents of wisdom," because the serpent biting his own tail formed the circle of wisdom, which was also an emblem of the spirit of life, or immortality. Kabalists assert that Chaos, Theos, Cosmos, are the three foundation-stones of space, that is, the embodiment of the unknown first cause. Therefore space is the body of the universe with its seven principles, and space is also called the "great sea." "And the earth was without form and void, and darkness was upon the face of the deep. And the

Spirit of God moved upon the face of the waters." Genesis.

The Gnostics were also called Ophites, or serpent worshipers. They were the first among the secret orders who divulged the arcane signification of the Jewish substitute for Ain-Soph, or the Absolute Silent One. They worshiped the serpent coiled around the sacramental loaf, which is the Egyptian Tau, and is in itself a phallic glyph. As the great serpent of space, or the dragon, it is the symbol of the manifested deity in its great wisdom; it is Sophia, the divine Sophia of the Gnostics. Still under another aspect, namely, that of the dual Androgyne, as a unit it is the Logos manifesting under a double principle of good and evil, because the serpent, or dragon, is the spirit of doubt or controversy which leads into inquiry, and results in knowledge. Therefore, when separated, the two Gnostic emblems typify the Tree of Life spiritual, and the Tree of Knowledge. Hence, Ophis is represented in Genesis as urging the first human couple, the production of matter, which is the source of evil, to eat the forbidden fruit, and become immortal: "Ye shall not surely die."

Egypt, the fountain source from which spring all our religious tenets, personified the soul of the world as an enormous serpent standing on human legs (Champollion). It is frequently portrayed with a beard in Gnostic engravings, and is identical with

Agathodemon, the good genius of the Ophites. The latter was endowed with knowledge of good and evil, and possessed divine wisdom. Iamblichus, and Champollion after him, have both recognized in Chnouphis, or the soul of the world, the great Thot Hermes, who was the occult personification of the celestial gods' fire. It is obviously the origin of the generic name of Thot Hermes, which was intimately linked with those of prophets, seers, and initiates. The latter were frequently called serpents of wisdom, because they were allegorically connected with the serpent, to whom is due their enlightenment through the solar and planetary gods of the earliest intellectual races. Moreover, Chnouphis was also the spiritual sun of enlightenment, and the patron of the Egyptian initiates, while, under the name of Bel-Merodach, the Chaldeans reverenced the same symbol, and denominated their adepts, Nebos, or Enochs. Any scholar who understands the name of Nebo will also perceive the reason why Moses disappears on Mount Nebo, and why his fiery serpents belong to the evil aspect of the dual Ophis.

Among the ancients the serpent was the most venerated symbol of their mysteries. As a representative of renewed life and immortality, it is met with on the doors of the chambers of the dead in the Egyptian and Chaldean tombs. Among the moderns it is yet a symbol of eternity in the bracelet of the fashionable woman for whom emblems are meaningless. It coils around the walking-stick in our days as it did in by-gone ages around the mythical tree. The Celestial Empire has preserved its great dragon, but the old Norse Sea kings' serpent is forgotten.

Draconis was the north pole, or the dragon of the North, identical with the fiery serpent that vivifies, while Hydra is the green dragon, or the water serpent of the South.

"The head and tail of the dragon, which represented the ascending and descending nodes of the moon, are also imaged as the two serpents that were strangled by the infant Hercules as soon as he was born. His nest, or cradle, was denoted by the twining serpents of the Caduceus, the head and tail of which were called the points of the ecliptic." The serpent typified the mystery of all mysteries, on account of its sloughing and self-renewal, which are considered to last three months, or the period of our winter solstice. Then the new-born solar god appeared and cut it in two, placing the two halves in heaven at the dividing point of the equinox. Such was also the significance of Moses' brazen serpent, with its rams' horns shaped in the form of a shining aureole, though the myth may be also interpreted as the lunar goddess, who reproduces the light, as the reflector and "Eye of Horus," or "Eye of Osiris." "Every astronomer besides occultists and astrologers knows that figuratively the astral light, the milky way, and also the path of the sun to the Tropics of Cancer and Capricorn, as well as the circles of the sidereal or tropical year, were always called 'serpents,' in the allegorical and mystic phraseology of the adepts."—*Secret Doctrine.* Christians themselves are reminded of the great wisdom inherent and acknowledged to have existed in the emblem of the serpent, by Jesus, who recommended his disciples " to be wise as serpents and harmless as doves."

The seven great planetary spirits are the agents of the seven stars of the Great Bear, who is the genitrix, Typhon, Set and even Apophis, the dragon killed by the solar god Horus. Under this aspect, it is the bad dragon, and as such he becomes the "dark side of Osiris," the contrast between light and darkness. The same system was adopted by the Greeks who depicted the abstract deity, Zeus, as a sublime conception, while the Olympic Zeus or Jove represents human intelligence in its lower aspect. The serpent Zeus tempts man, and in the course of time begets the solar Bacchus, who is the universal Christos, conceived and reproduced in the myths of every archaic nation. If we consider that Akasa, or the Astral Light, is the universal soul, that it fills space, and that without it there could be no manifested universe, we will conclude that it must be the cause of good and evil. "It is a fatal light which kills and destroys," says Eliphas Levi. And St. Paul exclaims: " It is sown a soul body, it is raised a spirit body."

And in another passage he refers to it as the "Prince of the air."

"Lead us not into temptation" is a terrible exhortation addressed by sinful man to his own sinful nature. There is no cause without effect, nor effect without a cause, therefore man himself generates the action of the great magic agent called the "Serpent of the Great Sea," or space. Ignorance is the cause of all wickedness, for should man know and understand that he is the creator of his own sufferings, he would certainly make strenuous efforts to conquer his evil tendencies. He would soon realize that knowledge is wisdom and not power, in the materialistic and wicked sense of the world.

"And he laid hold on the dragon, that old serpent, which is the devil and Satan, and bound him a thousand years. And cast him into the bottomless pit, and shut him up, and set a seal upon him, that he should deceive the nations no more till the thousand years should be fulfilled. And after that he must be loosed a little season." Revelation, chap. 20. Obviously this passage refers to the A-Draconis, which played false when it ceased to be the central point around which the starry heaven used to revolve, and which will be let loose again for a "little season," when the time comes for it to re-assume its old place, as the north pole's pivot.

In Syro-Chaldean occultism both Ophis and

Ophio-morphos, the good and the bad serpent or devil, are united in the Zodiac at the sign of the Androgyne Virgo-Scorpio, thus combining the emblem of life's duality of good and evil. Before its fall on earth the serpent was Ophis Chrestos, but after its fall it became Ophio-morphos Chrestos, or the evil principle.

CHAPTER VIII.

"THE SQUARE," "THE TREE," AND "THE MOUNT."

No. 4. "And before the throne there was a sea of glass like unto crystal; and in the midst of the throne and around about the throne, were four beasts, full of eyes before and behind." Revelation.

THE square typifies the earth in natural genesis, but in the Pythagorean phraseology it is an emblem of wisdom and intellect, when blended with the triangle. The secrets of all the mysteries contained in the sacred books, and expounded by the philosophical schools of ancient times, are unfolded, as we have stated frequently, not in words but in figures and numbers. Thus the mother, the first ancestor, who conveyed an idea of oneness to her children, is the great genitrix, the "mother of all," found in the genesis of every religion. It is the principle that differentiated, that manifested itself on the visible plane, while her progeny, the child, is the Androgyne typified by the calf of the Egyptians and the Hebrews (because it belongs to either sex): the Aleph or 1. The Latin word Vir was the triadic at puberty or figure 3, but the individual father was fourth, the figure of the tetrad. In this mythical way was established the principle of the esoteric division of monad (1), duad (2), triad (3), and tetrad (4); the Pythagorean explanation being: In what you conceive four there are ten, a perfect triangle and our oath. The Hebrew Sheba or oath being 7, thus: 1, 2, 3, 4 = 10, or the letter yod, the full number of Iao-Sabaoth. The cult of the Roman Church was established upon the symbolism of the mother with her child of the early races; it is the reason why God the Father is absent from the Christian monuments anterior to the thirteenth century. The principal opponents to the paternal deity were the Gnostics, who exalted Sophia, the genitrix of ancient nations, together with her child, Horus. The latter became, later on, the anointed Messiah. Thus, the meaning of the triangle was easily understood; but the tetrad, or the fourfold nature of the one god or divine unity, became a mystery for the followers of the Pope. The survival of this iconography is still continued in the square Nimbus, with which God the Father is represented, though this symbol has become meaningless to the worshipers of Mary and her child Jesus.

The Gnostics asserted that their science rested on a square, the angles of which represented respectively sige (silence), bythos (depth), nous (spiritual soul or mind), and aletheia (truth).

In Revelation, chap. iv, we read: "And before the throne there was a sea of glass like unto crystal; and in the midst of the throne and round about the throne, were four beasts full of eyes before and behind.

"And the first beast was like a lion, and the second beast like a calf, and the third beast had a face as a man, and the fourth beast was like a flying eagle."

This passage of Revelation corresponds to the same subject as described in Ezekiel's vision of the cherubim: "And their whole body and their backs, and their hands, and their wings, and the wheels, were full of eyes round about, even the wheels that they four had.

"As for the wheels, it was cried unto them in my hearing, O wheel! And every one had four faces; the first face was the face of a cherub, and the second the face of a man, and the third the face of a lion, and the fourth the face of an eagle." These four symbolical creatures were identical with the four protecting genii of the Assyrians, who were in the human likeness, but with a bull's head, a lion's body, a man's face, an eagle's head, and a complete human being. They are the typical four corners or four angles. Under another aspect they symbolize the four elements, and also the four lower principles in man. Astronomically, they represent the four constellations which accompany the solar god, and occupy during the winter solstice the four corners, or cardinal points, of the zodiacal circle.

The same emblems of Ezekiel's vision and John's revelation are handed down to us in the symbolical pictures of the four evangelists, Matthew, Mark, Luke and John, with their respective man, lion, ox and eagle.

THE SQUARE, TREE, AND MOUNT. 135

The first triangle of the Pythagorean triad, Chaos, Theos, Cosmos, or the god of the three aspects, was transformed, through its perfect quadrature of the infinite circle, into the four-faced Brahma.

The square, as the symbol of the earth and of material life, is linked with the different emblems of reproduction, or generation. As number 4, its significance is generally associated with the Jewish god Jehovah, the god of the four letters, as explained in the Kabala. In this case it becomes a phallic emblem. Thus I is Yod, the membrum virile, H is Hé, the womb; V is Vau, and is synonymous of crook, hook, and nail, and the fourth letter H means also an opening; consequently the four letters composing the name Jehovah are a bisexual emblem expressing the male and female symbol. Therefore, Jehovah esoterically is a dual conception, embodying an antagonistic principle, namely, a spiritual and a material element; and as such it is good and bad because it is spirit and matter. The former is the source of all goodness, the latter the origin of all evil. The tutelary divinity of the Jews was one of the three lowest Elohim who generated physical man. He is essentially a moon-god, and under this latter aspect he is not the A O of a neuter gender, under which sign the non-virile god was typified. The latter has survived to our present day, and is to be found among the votaries of the Roman Catholic Church who wear the sign of the woman on their head, and the frock of the female down to their feet. Such is the origin of the tonsure, which priests and monks exhibit as a sign that they belong to the neutral gender.

Religious sects have vied with each other in their efforts to display upon their sacred monuments the outward signs of Phallicism, while in India the Linga and Yoni are profusely adorning the most stately temples and mausoleums; in Europe graceful steeples, designated upon the same pattern, rise above cathedrals and churches alike; and testify, jointly with the domes, cupolas, and round towers of the Mahometans, to the survival of sexual symbology, and the universal acceptance of its emblems.

The phenomenal world received its culmination with the evolution of man, who is the mystic square, in his metaphysical aspect. The Tetractis, the most sacred Quaternion, is number 36, or the decans of the four quarters. It was the most sacred oath among the Egyptians, who called it the "Word." Hence, the fourfold god, who united the monad, duad, triad in the unity of a tenfold totality, was the fourfaced Brahma among the Hindus, and God the Father, with a four-cornered Nimbus, among the Christians. Truly, number 10, the Pythagorean decade, was considered as the "Begetter of souls," but the power of ten was said to reside in number 4.

Number 36, which is expressed by the decans of the Zodiac, is intimately linked with the seventh sign of the Zodiac. In fact, the Hindus render the word Tula, which corresponds to our own balance or Libra, as 36. They explain that the manifesting deity is encased within the decans of the four quarters, and that the fourth Zodiacal division, the crab, should be represented thus, IIII, their intent being evidently to connect it with the sacred Tetragram. It is obvious that 36 being 9 tetraktis, 12 triads or 3 duodecahedrons, should have been considered as the most sacred number by Pythagoreans and Kabalists.

In "Raphael's Disputa" God the Father also wears the square disk, as a continuation of the emblem of his fourfold nature, and in Belshazzar's dream the same myth is typified in the four metals: gold, silver, brass, and iron mixed with clay, with reference to periods.

The Tetragrammaton, the Adam Kadmon of the Kabalists, is also called the "heavenly man of the four letters," and as such he is considered by some as the creative deity mentioned in the first chapter of Genesis. But whether we consider him as a quaternary, tetragrammaton, or a triad, the biblical Elohim is not the universal Ten, unless blended with Ain-Soph, the Non-Being. He is only one of the many septenaries of the universal septenate. The word "he" is not correct either, as the creative god of Genesis was not masculine.

The first tree was at the center of the circle as

the symbol of reproduction, the mother of life. It was also an emblem of knowledge, and as such became one of the great allegories of the Mosaic books. The tree of the Paradise is the true intelligencer to men—"in the day ye eat thereof then your eyes shall be opened, and ye shall be as gods, knowing good and evil. Genesis, chapter 3. The "serpent" who pronounced those words was not the theological Satan, but one of the Elohim, who, like the beneficent Prometheus of the Greeks, wished to lead man on the road to immortality. When he retorted to the woman, "Ye shall not surely die," he referred only to his incorruptible nature. This bright angel was the chief of the Androgyne creators who removed the veil of ignorance which prevented the angelic man to perceive his own nakedness: "And the eyes of them both were opened, and they knew that they were naked; and they sewed fig leaves together, and made themselves aprons." Man had not yet fallen into generation; he was still the boneless god of the early races, but was waking to the consciousness of his real nature and becoming more material. "Unto Adam also and to his wife did the Lord God make coats of skins and clothed them." Which passage answers entirely to the Quiché manuscript, "For so far men had no flesh," the same traditions having been preserved among archaic races.

The fall, really, can be only interpreted as the

action of differentiating consciousness on the various planes of our universe, or world. It is the rebellion of spirit who seeks union with matter, while the angels with the flaming swords typify the animal passions inherent in the human nature. The latter are so many stumbling-blocks in the way to acquire the tree of knowledge (or wisdom). The Adam, driven from the Paradise, typifies the newly separated race, our own fourth race, who abused and dragged the mystery of life into such a degree of bestiality as to cause man to be regarded in this respect as inferior to animals.

In the "Secret Doctrine" we read: "Creative powers in man were the gift of divine wisdom, not the result of sin—nor was the curse of Karma called down upon them for seeking natural union, as all the mindless animal world does at the proper season, but for abusing the creative power, for desecrating the divine gift and wasting the life-essence for no purpose, except bestial personal gratification. When understood, the third chapter of Genesis will be found to refer to the Adam and Eve of the closing third and the commencing fourth races. Nature has never intended that woman should bring forth her young ones in sorrow. Since that period, during the evolution of the fourth race, there came enmity between its seed and the serpent's seed, the seed or product of Karma and divine wisdom. For the seed, or woman of lust, bruised the head of the seed of the fruit of wisdom and knowledge by turning the holy mystery of procreation into animal gratification."

"Prometheus, who robbed fire from heaven, is older than the Hellenes, for it belongs in truth to the dawn of human consciousness. Prometheus means, 'He who sees before him,' he robs the gods, the Elohim of their secret, the mystery of the creative fire. For this sacrilegious attempt he is struck down by Kronos (time) and delivered into Zeus, the father and creator of a mankind which he would wish to have blind intellectually and animal-like, a personal deity which will not see man "like one of us." Hence Prometheus, the fire, the light-giver, is chained on Mount Caucasus and condemned to suffer torture. But the triform fates (Karma) whose decrees, as the Titan says, even Zeus cannot escape, ordain that those sufferings will last only to that day when a son is born. This son will deliver Prometheus (suffering humanity) from his own fatal gift. His name is, "He who has to come." This points to cyclic transformations, to the opposite arc of the cycle, when human progeny was created, not begotten." The Jews used to teach that to reveal the secrets of the Kabala was like eating the fruit of the tree of knowledge, it was punishable with the severest penalty, even death.

The tree of knowledge of the manuscript describing the mysteries among the Mayas and the Quichés contains an engraving of a tree analogous to the Kabalistic Sephirothal tree. The tree is shaped like a T, or Egyptian Tau, its trunk is covered with ten fruits ready to be plucked by a male and a female standing on each side. Each shooting branch of the Tau bears a triple branch with a bird, emblem of immortality, sitting between the two, and forming the perfect number 7. As in the Sephirothal tree, we count ten in all and seven without the upper triad. The ten fruits born out of the two invisible male and female make up twelve, the Pythagorean Dodecahedron of the universe.

The tree typifies renewal and reproduction and also spiritual rebirth, therefore it was linked with the celebration of the mysteries in which the adept was regenerated and born again. Many of the ancient deities embodied this idea. Isis found the Ark of Osiris exposed on the Nile, containing the child entangled in a thicket of tamarisk, which completely inclosed both the child and the ark within its trunk, and grew up into a stately tree.

Hathor, in the shape of the sycamore tree, is the emblem of the shrine of the child. Under this aspect the tree becomes an emblem of reproduction; forsooth, it degenerates into a phallic glyph, and is denounced by the Jewish prophets in vehement language. The tree, as the foreteller, or oracle, was held in high esteem; as, for example, the oak tree of Dodona, the sacred palm of Negra in Yemen, the Ava tree of the Polynesian, the Seyba tree of Central America, and many other venerated trees. Among the Jews the idea was synthesized in a living woman who was worshiped under the branches of the tree. Isaiah, referring to those rites, denounces the "Sons of Sorcerers" who inflame themselves with idols under every green tree; and Jeremiah, reproving the same customs, says of Israel: "She is gone up upon every high mountain and under every green tree and there hath played the harlot." According to Hosea they sacrificed under the tree "because the shadow thereof was good." The tree was also the hill-altar of the Jews, upon which they offered their propitiatory sacrifice. "His own self bare our sins in his own body on the tree." (Peter.) It is claimed that Buddha has been re-incarnated forty or fifty times under the tree of knowledge (or wisdom). He is represented as standing under the Bo-tree. The Eastern sages declare that the tree of knowledge in the Paradise of man's own heart becomes the tree of life eternal, and has naught to do with man's animal senses; but the tree worship of the Jews must have been very different, if we judge from the manner their prophets reproved them.

A reminiscence of the mythical tree is found in the gooseberry bush of England, under which the babies are found. It is the typical bearer of fruit, because the tree yields the fruit. But the symbolism attached to the tree depends also a great deal upon the species to which it belongs. For example, the palm tree, as the producer of the milk, was rather a glyph embodying an early type of supplying a want; while under another aspect, as in the Quiché Ballet, and in the beak of Noah's dove, the palm indicated a new period of manifestation of matter after a destructive cataclysm. The fig-tree, the lotus, the pomegranate, are all phallic emblems; they are synonymous with womb, because they contain their seed within themselves. Several ancient nations portrayed the genitrix, the type of motherhood, in the tree, the coins of ancient Crete being an illustration thereof. In Central America there is still in circulation a small silver coin, called cuartillo, with a Seiba on one side, and in the Quiché manuscript of Chichicastenango we are told that the second attempt at creating a perfect physical man resulted in a wooden man and a woman made of the marrow of cibak (reed). Hor Apollo asserts that the Egyptians, to show ancient descent, depicted a bundle of papyrus, because the root was eaten as food and the plant was used to make the book. Such seems to be the origin of the expression in Revelation: "And I took the little book out of the angel's hand and ate it up, and it was in my mouth sweet as honey, and as soon as I had eaten it, my belly was bitter." Here the book that is eaten up is equivalent with receiving knowledge and information from the tree that tells, the producer of food, both material and spiritual. That such an interpretation was understood is corroborated by the assertion that the word education meant Sheba in Egyptian, which is synonymous with sufficient food. Thus Elohim exclaims, "Behold the man is become as one of us!" The tree had taught them how to discern good from evil, and Elohim, the elementary gods of Genesis, were jealous of the knowledge he had acquired. The tree that confers spiritual sight is also typified in the Soma, Homa, and many other drinks that induce a state of trance. Even the Jews were ordered to spend their savings in drink, as expressed in Deuteronomy, chapter 14: "And thou shalt bestow that money for whatsoever thy soul lusteth after, for oxen, or for sheep, or for wine, or for strong drink, or for whatsoever thy soul desireth; and thou shalt eat there before the Lord thy God, and thou shalt rejoice, thou, and thine household." This passage undoubtedly refers to a religious rite. But in the Rig-Veda, even the gods are represented as getting drunk on an immortal stimulant, which bestows immortality upon them. The Mexican genitrix Mayaquil is changed by the gods into the maguey, the plant that produces the native wine, showing the universality of this myth. But the Egyptians connected the wine more especially with the fall of the angels, or giants, the opponents of light, and as such considered it as a cause of the sin against nature. It was the cause of human depravity, for through it spirit became intoxicated. It plunged into such lawlessness that it called for divine vengeance. The fall, however, can be explained astronomically and mystically. Under the last aspect, wine is the blood of the tree of life, which was partaken of in the eucharist of the mysteries, original type of the Christian communion ceremony. Moreover, the root of the Greek word Sophia, or wisdom, comes from the Egyptian Kep or Sep, the spirit of wine and sap. The juice can be traced to Sapiens, the whole agreeing with the source that typifies knowledge, namely, the tree of Life.

The glyph, most intimately linked with the tree, is the mount. It is considered equivalent to the point in the center of the circle, as the beginning, or starter. It is a primordial type of the genitrix under the type of the mount of the North, which is also the birthplace of the beginning. Frequent references are made to both the mount and the tree in the Old and in the New Testament. St. Paul says in Corinthians, chapter 10: "And did all drink the same spiritual drink, for they drank of that Spiritual Rock that followed them, and that rock was Christ." And again in Galatians, chapter 4: "For it is written that Abraham had two sons, the one by a bond-maid, the other by a free woman. But he who was of the bondwoman was born after the flesh; but he of the free woman was by promise. Which things are an allegory, for these are the two covenants, the one from the Mount Sinai, which gendereth to bondage, which is Agar. For this Agar is Mount Sinai in Arabia, and answereth to Jerusalem which now is, and is in bondage with her children. But Jerusalem which is above is free, which is the mother of us all. "If we bear in mind that every patriarchal name found in the Bible refers to either geological periods or races we may infer that Paul, who belonged to the class of itinerant thereapeutics or healers, whose seat was at Alexandria, was familiar with the symbolical nature attributed to the mount. For does he not declare that Jerusalem is the "mother of us all." It is certainly an allusion to the great mother, typified by the mount. It is identical with the rock, or mount, which, under the name of the "Bad Woman" of Hong Kong, presides over the illicit intercourse of sexes, a degraded emblem of the original glyph under its primeval aspect. St. Paul has bequeathed the same symbol to the Christians, in his epistle to Timothy, in which he likens the church to a house, and a pillar as basis of the truth. Thus all the primitive myths of the Mount, Tree, Seat, Pillar and Abode are synthesized in the mother church.

The Old Testament is not lacking in examples illustrating the prevalence of the same conceptions: "And Jacob set up a pillar in the place where he talked with him, even a pillar of stone, and he poured a drink-offering thereon, and he poured oil thereon." Jacob's pillar is evidently the lingham of the Hindus, for in this case the monument befittingly becomes the deity who has just ordered him: "Be fruitful and multiply; a nation and a company of nations shall be of thee; and kings shall come out of thy loins." So did Isis pour perfumed oil upon it and wrap it in fine linen preparatory to depositing it in her temple, and such was the source of the worship of Priapus. The usual symbol of the phallus was an erect stone, either in its rough state or sculptured. Remnants of it can be found the world over.

Hesiod in his Theogony insinuates that the occult meaning underlying the myth of the sacred tree and the rock, is of too deep import to babble it to the vulgar. Max Muller says, in a flippant way, that the Hebrews speak of the "Rock of Israel," in a sense entirely absent in the Homeric text, but such an assertion is ridiculous, because the typology is exactly the same. In both cases it is the Rock from which man sprung, and the interpretation must be similar. To it we will presently trace back the word Sacrament, a survival of the ancient mysteries. Symbologists and Hebrew scholars have proven that the passage, "in the image of God created he him," is in the original text Sacr, and n' cabvah-phallus and yoni, the emblem under which the Lord God appeared to his chosen people. Jehovah said to Moses, "The summation of my name is Sacr, the carrier of the germ," the equivalent for phallus. It is the same symbol as the lily in the hand of Gabriel, which is typical of the Annunciation, and is synonymous with the sacraments of the Christians.

Finally, the tree is the type of the pole of heaven.

It is identical with the tripod, and the tree depicted by Lajard in his "Culte de Mithra." In this case it is accompanied by the sun, moon and seven stars. The Christmas-tree is a reminiscence of the tree of life.

CHAPTER IX.

THE CROSS.

"And out of his mouth goeth a sharp sword, that with it he should smite the nations; and he shall rule them with a rod of iron; and he treadeth the wine-press of the fierceness and wrath of Almighty God."—*St. John's Revelation.*

PLATO, who flourished 348 years before the Christian era, records that the Egyptian priests pointed out to him, on their pyramids, the symbolical hieroglyphics of a religion which had existed in uninterrupted orthodoxy among them for upwards of ten thousand years. That emblem was the cross, the most sacred glyph of Egyptian worship. It stood on all obelisks and pyramids as a representative of "life eternal," and every planet was imagined as accompanied by a cross. The monogram of the god Saturn was the sign of the cross, together with a ram's horn, hence identifying him with the Lamb of God, or the Christian Christ. To the present day, Jupiter bears a cross with a crescent or horn underneath. Venus is depicted as a cross below a circle. Mercury unites the moon, the circle, and the cross. Mars has an oblique cross with a circle. Therefore one of the phases under which the cross must be interpreted is designated as the astronomical cross.

This emblem, together with the Tau or crux ansata, was most conspicuous, not only in Egypt and India, but also in Central America and Southern Mexico. Krishna's temples, like the most celebrated of our Gothic cathedrals, are built in the form of the cross. Among the ancients the tree was frequently shaped into the form of a cross with four oscilla hanging from its branches. Our Christmas-trees have derived their significance from the original type of the "*feeder*," but have lost their arcane attributes by the dropping of the four pendants which were related to the four cardinal points, and linked the cross-shaped tree to the mother of revolutions, "Ursa Major." She was the first to describe the circle in the heavens. As the spirit of life and immortality was synthesized by the circle, the serpent biting his tail portrayed the circle of wisdom in infinity, and so did the astronomical cross, or the cross within a circle.

The cross also indicates the union of spirit with matter, and as such becomes a phallic symbol, *i. e.*, the masculine tree of life, or the fourfold phallus and the Egyptian Tat or Tau. This latter symbol is the Ru, Rosary, or feminine sign blended with the fourfold linga, which is one of the most conspicuous types of primitive symbology, and belongs to the early imagery preserved in the long-horned Cairn. The same shape of the uterus within, and the four horns at the corners, was the pattern upon which the mound-builders erected their tombs.

The cross was a most venerated emblem among the ancient Egyptians, because it was associated with the beneficent river, the Nile. The inundations of the Nile alone bring fertility to lower Egypt, and without them the whole country would be a barren desert. Therefore transverse beams shaped like a cross were erected at the spots where the water was expected to rise the most. They became, in the course of time, objects of veneration, essentially linked with terrestrial life, and the mysterious occult side of nature. The Nile was an Egyptian deity, and the crosses were emblems of abundance and blessing. For was not the flood itself the sign of the waters of life? Thus the cross portrayed material life. But as the Egyptians were great astronomers, they were able to predict beforehand the exact time of the inundation, and to connect that most important event with the movements and phases of the heavenly bodies. Hence, the astronomical cross was also the Egyptian Tau. For, was not the first circle quartered according to the four cardinal points? That is the true derivation of the quarter, or fourth part, as a way of dividing. The same system is continued in our heraldry, in what is denominated the quartering of arms.

In the Bible we find frequent references to the sign of the cross. We read in Ezekiel, chapter 2: "And the Lord said unto him, Go through the midst of the city, through the midst of Jerusalem, and set a mark upon the foreheads of the men that sigh, and that cry for all the abominations that be done in the midst thereof." The mark here is obviously the sign of the cross.

And again in St. John's Revelation: "And after these things I saw four angels, standing on the four corners of the earth, holding the four winds of the earth, that the wind should not blow on the earth, nor on the sea, nor on any tree.

"And I saw another angel ascending from the east, having the seal of the living God; and he cried with a loud voice to the four angels, to whom it was given to hurt the earth and the sea, saying Hurt not the earth, neither the sea, nor the trees, till we have sealed the servants of our God in their foreheads."

The cross being the type of the four elements, synonymous with the four cardinal points, the four corners or angles, the four angels of the squared circle here mark, brand, or seal with the sign of the cross, the primitive token applied to those who had reached a culminating point, that had just been crossed.

In all engravings and pictures recovered from the Egyptians the sacred Tau holds a foremost part. Neophytes and hierophants alike carry it in their hands during the ceremonials of initiation, and have it besides embroidered upon their vestments It was traced with oil upon the forehead of the aspirant to initiation, as it is now continued in like manner in the Roman Catholic Churches and other Christian churches, as a part of the ceremonies of baptism and confirmation. It images in each case spiritual rebirth, the descent into hell, and the ascent again into the heavenly kingdom, typified by the passage of the sun across the line of the ecliptic. It also indicates the evolution of the manifesting deity, and is a universal glyph embodying the sexual duality, or male and female principles It is stamped upon the great celestial book of the starry heavens, shining brilliantly as the southern cross.

When the sun entered the sign of Aries, the old Typhon or Dragon was superseded by the Lamb or Ram, and the Egyptian and Persian typologists adopted that emblem as the symbol of the Saviour of the world, as early as the year 2410 B. C. It was not until the end of the seventh century that the fathers of the council of Trullo proclaimed that the Lamb should be replaced by Jesus Christ, our man-god. But in the Christian iconography the cross is inseparable of the Ram and the Lamb as a glory, or under other forms of accompaniment. Moreover, the fish is found forever associated with the symbolical Christ.

We must bear in mind that the letters of the Hebrew alphabet have a numerical value under which the real occult meaning of the sacred Scriptures is constantly concealed. For example, our Adamic race begins, in Kabalistic reckonings, when the sun was in the sign of the Bull, which event took place when the sign of the Scorpion was opposite. Now, scholars translate the word scorpion into "instrument of perdition," and connect this zodiacal sign with the fall of the first couple. Of course we are well aware that there was no first man, but we know positively that the scorpion belongs to the phallic glyphs, and consequently is one of the types under which the fall into generation has been represented. Moreover, the Bull is Aleph, or I, which △ is also the sign of the concealed deity, or △. The sum of the words Jehovah and the Bull is 532, a most remarkable number in astronomical science; for the Hebrews believed that the "Eye of the Bull," Aldebaran, was directed towards the unknown deity Jehovah, who is quite well identified now.

The ancients recognized the Ram as the successor to the Bull, hence the Jewish lamb of the passover and our divine Lamb or Christ. This sign corresponds to the balance or scales, synthesis of justice. This idea was illustrated in the child of the zodiac of Denderah, who represented the River Nile and the descending sun, and was seated on the scales at the crossing. In another zodiac, the oblong zodiac of Denderah, Horus is portrayed on the top of a mountain with the balance over his head. In several other zodiacs the balance is found in union with the Nilometer, which indicated the full flood and lowest ebb, and was the cross or tree of life. Such is the origin of the Christian festival of the exaltation of the holy cross, and the invention of the cross. The church celebrates the hiding as a corollary of the finding of the cross. In no country of the world is this festival celebrated with more enthusiasm than in Central America and Mexico.

For 2,155 years the lamb or ram was to the ancients the Christ of that particular circle of time. Among the Hindus, Agni, the spirit or Fire, whose emblem is a fiery cross, is portrayed riding on the young ram as the solar sign of re-birth; and the Egyptian solar deities wear a ram's head. The same emblem of the cross and the lamb is continued to the present day. The Catholic priests when officiating frequently wear garments upon which the lamb is embroidered carrying the cross, and they offer him as a sacrificial victim, who "takes away the sins of the world."

When the equinox passed into the sign of Pisces the emblematic fish became interwoven with the mythical Christ on the cross. Our Christian era really dates from the day that our sun was ushered into the zodiacal sign of Pisces. In fact, the Greek word "fish" has been rendered "Jesus Christ, Son of God Saviour," by using each letter of the Greek word "fish" as initial letter for each word composing the above sentence. Moreover, the virgin is the zodiacal sign corresponding to Pisces. We find the symbolical Pisces sculptured upon the ancient stones of the catacombs, and in many churches and chapels. They are a well-known theological emblem. The Christ and the fish are intimately linked together; the Christ was crucified on Friday, and the Catholics eat fish on Friday, both suffering the penalty of death on the same day. They typify the resurrection from the dead for the souls since the year 155 B. C., the Christ hanging on the cross, and the two fishes tied with a ribbon and suspended, being synonymous in the ancient ideography. The hanging or suspension of the Nile waters at the time of the summer solstice, when the flood had reached its greatest height, lasted fifteen days according to a Coptic tradition, and is still kept in remembrance by the cross that is flung into the waters in St. Petersburg, and the blessing of the waters among Christians. But that cross was essentially the Nile cross, indicating the re-birth of the first Horus from the waters. He is identical with St. John. As the waters went on decreasing, the sun also dwindled away slowly to re-appear nine months afterwards as the fire or sun of resurrection, at the vernal equinox. St. John has expressed the same conception in these words: "He that cometh after me is preferred before me; for he was before me." Hence, the mythos keeps record of two Horuses and two Christs, even in the Christian symbology.

One of the most interesting explanations of the mysterious way in which records were preserved in antiquity, is the following borrowed from the "Se-

THE CROSS. 157

cret Doctrine:" "When Moses asked Jehovah to show him his glory, he showed him his back, *i. e.*, his manifested universe." "Thou canst not see my face, but thou shalt see me behind." If we bear in mind that Jehovah has been identified as the personification of the moon, we will easily comprehend that he could be represented in numbers as the lunar year. Well, now the corner of 543, which means "I" (21) am (501) "I" (21), and the behind would make 345, or the face; the riddle being thus solved, and they saw each other face to face. Still another combination of the two quantities, $345 + 543 = 888$, is the Gnostic value for the name Christ, who was also Joshua, Jehoshua, or the sun. The same result of the 888 would be found by dividing the 24 hours of the day; it would also give 3 times number 8 for a quotient.

In the myth, the sun and the moon are the father and mother of the Christ. Even in Revelation the woman who brings forth a child is arrayed with the sun, and has the moon under her feet. The same symbology has been preserved in Christian iconography, many mementoes of the ancient ideal being still extant in which, at the conjunction of the sun and moon, the young solar god appears as at his birth at Easter. The festival of the resurrection is still determined by the full moon, as it was in Egypt ages ago.

There are many differently shaped crosses; they are all well represented in ecclesiastical blazonry, but most promiscuously in the Roman Catholic hierarchy. Thus, to the bishop is assigned the single cross; to the archbishop and cardinals, the double cross; and to the Pope belongs the sixfold cross.

The word cardinal comes from the word cardo, a point or nick of time, and the cross is the cardinal points of the circle, thus: for the cross and the circle are insepara- ble in symbology. The sixfold cross of the Pope was a feminine aspect of the cross, standing in close relation with number 666 of the beast of Revelation, or the S. S. S., which is a form of the cross-bearer Sistrum, and one of the dual phallic emblems combining the union of the male with the female principle. The same imagery is continued in the perpetual lamp burning forever before the altar. Moreover, the Pope wears the miter shaped like the fishes' mouth, as an inheritance of the Genitrix of Rome, whose peculiar head-gear it had been for centuries.

An ancient typical custom among Roman Catholics, is the one of creeping on all fours to the cross on Good Friday. In many provinces in Europe the custom has not died out yet. The present writer has witnessed many times, in several rural towns, the whole congregation creeping on all fours to the cross and kissing it on the four extremities, ignorantly marking the four typical corners of heathen times. The egg, as the circle, was also associated with the cross, so that when money was not collected near the cross, the eggs were received as an offering, and the two were blended into a perfect symbol of ancient ideography under the eyes of the ignorant worshipers. Thus far we have conclusively proven that if the Jews borrowed of the Egyptians "jewels of silver, and jewels of gold, and raiment" (which means they plagiarized the symbolical teachings of their masters: "And the Lord gave the people favor in the sight of the Egyptians, so that they lent unto them such things as they required. And they spoiled the Egyptians." Exodus, chapter 12) the Christians followed their example centuries after the exodus.

It is claimed that Thot invented the Egyptian alphabet, and the letter Tau, which is an equivalent to the cross. " T " is placed at the end of the Hebrew and Samaritan alphabet. With them it typified the end of a thing, and the perfection, security, and culmination of things. The great Masonic author, Ragon, asserts that the letter T, or the Tau, was synonymous with terminus, and roof, which implies an idea of shelter, refuge, security.

Of all the differently-shaped crosses the Svastica, or Swastica, called also the jaina-cross by the Masons, is one of the most mystic glyphs of occult science. The missionaries of India call it the devil's cross, because it shines on the seven-headed serpent of Vishnu, and on the thousand-headed Ananta, as represented in the depths of the Indian hell. But why do they interpret this personification of cycles of time and eternity, in a common and literal manner? Has not St. Paul taught publicly, and left in writing, that the letter killeth? Has he not said in his chapter on the sacraments of the Jews that the "Rock of which they drank was Christ"? Why then not explain intelligently the mysteries of other creeds? The Svastica is so profoundly philosophical that the one who should meditate on its attributes would learn the secret of the evolution of worlds and man. Associated with the Workers' Hammer of the book of Numbers, it is the "Hammer which striketh sparks from the flint," illustrating graphically the process of evolving worlds. It is also Thor's Hammer of the Norse legend, which was forged by the dwarfs to be used against the Titans, or pre-cosmic forces of nature. The Svastica is a symbol pregnant with deep meaning. The Masons have adopted it as the gavel or mallet of the grand Master Masons, regardless of its many-sided interpretations. In the Jaina-cross can be found the solution of the divine and human cycle of science, for it is the Alpha and Omega of creative force, beginning on the spiritual plane and ending in the abyss of matter. It is the link between heaven and earth; one arm is raised towards heaven, while the other one points to the earth, synthesizing the union of spirit with matter.

The Svastica, as a sign of life, was also a phallic

symbol expressed by a double Z, which denoted generation as portrayed by four hooks. The "fiery serpents" of the Hebrews sprung from the same idea, for were they not raised on a cross-pole, or Stauros? Moreover, the Svastica was a universal symbol ages before the Christians adopted the Latin cross as an emblem. The Svastica has been discovered under the ruined monuments of ancient Egypt, on the prehistoric pottery of Cyprus, in Ireland, England, and is now conspicuous still in India as a form of the cross to which an occult significance is attached. One of the Svastica crosses found in the catacombs has the following inscription: "Vitalis, Vitalia, Life of Life." From the Svastica originated the custom of eating hot cross buns on good Friday, and of blessing the "Cross Candle," which is still dipped into holy water. But a few years ago the present writer has seen French peasants *"lighting up the thunder," that is, lighting blessed candles which had been sanctified by praying and dipping them into the water on Saturday following Good Friday. In this case, it was an attempt to re-establish harmony among the powers of above. It was a sort of preventative against evil.

The Mexican crosses were also symbols of rain or water, the idea of rain and cross seeming inseparable, though the four elements are also typified in the cross, and more particularly in the decussated cross. The latter as X points to the four

---
* During a storm.

cardinal points, uniting the divine with the human principle, the finite with the infinite. It begins at the junction, the crossing, and loses itself in the boundless space. The Christian cross is the final phase of an emblem derived from the heathen world, and the Roman Emperor Julian was right when he exclaimed, "I wage a warfare with the X!" It is still a sign of multiplication among us, as it was ages ago; it is yet the conjunction of two that results in an increase. Neither has its meaning changed since St. John's Revelation was published to the world. It is still "the sharp sword that with it he should smite the nations," for the hilt of the sword has drunk more of the human life in Christian missionary expeditions than any other death instrument. Moreover, the original type of the crossing of the sun through the ecliptic, is still maintained, as well as its re-birth in the vernal equinox. "And he shall rule them with a rod of iron," continued to be the motto of our sun, whose history is preserved in the mythical records of the Christ and the cross.

Until the so-called conversion of Constantine the Great, the Labarum, or royal standard, bore the monogram K. R. of the Kronian, or solar cross, identical with the emblem under which the victorious solar god was imaged in the pagan ideography. After Constantine's victory he is portrayed as the conqueror with a cross overhead, and the dragon writhing at his feet. It was a repetition of the custom adopted by the Pharaohs, who impersonated the god during certain festivals; which custom must have been prevalent among the ancient civilized nations of America, because the same emblem has been found in the sculptures of Palenque. No miracle was necessary to repeat a phase of ancient mysteries. Constantine had committed fearful crimes for which the pagan priests had no atonement to offer. Sopater, the heathen priest, friend of Constantine, assured him that the "purity of the gods admitted of no compromise with sin," whereupon Constantine applied to the bishops of the Christian faith, and they promised him that "by repentance and baptism they could cleanse him from all sins." Such is the authenticated cause of Constantine's conversion, and of the substitution of the Kronian cross for the Christian cross.

The cross has a sevenfold meaning, as linked with the phenomena of light, heat, electricity, terrestrial magnetism, astral radiation, motion, and intelligence, or self-consciousness. It is the source of life of all things, and has been identified with the mystery of re-birth, either materially or spiritually speaking, by the nations of the remotest antiquity.

The Christ on the cross was an after-thought of the Christian Fathers, who thus materialized the metaphysical conceptions of the ancients. The first crucifix, with a figure, or Christ, on it, was gotten up by Pope Gregory the Great, as a present to

Queen Theodolinde, of Lombardy, about the seventh century of our era. It is now to be found in the Church of St. John at Monza, as a curious specimen of early Christian art, whilst the catacombs, the hidden place in which the early worshipers of the personal Christ are supposed to have treasured the relics of their cult, contain only mementoes of the Egyptian symbology. No man-Christ is represented, but the cross is associated with the lamb, the dove, the palm, the fish and even the phallus! The image of the Gnostic Christ, the Christian Horus of Egyptian origin, is the youthful sun-god of the vernal equinox portrayed as entering the sign of Pisces with the crocodile under his feet. (See frontispiece.)

St. Paul, referring to the natural and occult interpretation of the mystery of blood spilling, says: "And to Jesus, the Mediator of the new covenant, and to the blood of sprinkling, that speaketh better things than that of Abel." Now, Abel typifying the first virgin blood spilled in the act of generation, is emblematic of the natural process of rebirth, but the esoteric interpretation, the spiritual re-birth, "speaketh better things." And in chapter 6 of the epistle to the Romans: " Therefore we are buried with him by baptism into death, that like as Christ was raised up from the dead by the glory of the Father, even so we also should walk in newness of life." St. Paul by applying the astronomical feat of the dying Horus, who has to cross the river of the Waterman in the heavens, and be baptized in its waters, has unwittingly contributed like other misunderstood therapeutists to the establishment of the sacramental rite of baptism.

In the initiation, the neophyte used to be tied to a couch in the shape of an Egyptian Tau, and at the end of three days and three nights he was carried from the temple crypt to the entrance of the gallery, at a spot where the early beams of the rising sun would strike full upon his face. The initiate was re-born, after his crucifixion upon the tree of life, after the manner of the youthful Horus. This pagan ceremony was not unknown to St. Paul, who says, after true heathen fashion: " Knowing this, that our old man is crucified with him, that the body of sin might be destroyed, that henceforth we should not serve sin." The expression among initiates is "to be crucified before the sun," and not against the sun.

The sculptured crucifixion discovered by Stephens among the Palenque ruins, is too well known to require another description. We allude to it simply to point out the universality of the same myth. Only ignorance has created a personal Christ, and only deception is keeping such a delusion as a verity before the public. Scholars have always admitted that the Word, Christ, or Logos, was a metaphysical conception of the ancients. Plato describes the Creator as making the universe of a spherical form, the most like unto his own shape. When therefore he cogitated over that god who was destined to exist at some certain period of time (which period was annual), he produced his body according to this same pattern, and the perfect circle of the created god he decussated in the shape of the letter X, which is the decussated cross.

The Catholic priest who shaves the crown of his head in imitation of the "glory," or who passes his head through the pallium or chasuble, personifies the male cross within the female circle, one of the primitive emblems of phallic symbology. The idea is borrowed from the Egyptians, who expressed the same glyph with the Tau in conjunction with the Ro. thus ☥. It is the source whereof sprung the doctrine of the Immaculate Conception, which had been kept secret for eighteen centuries, and was promulgated to the Catholic world in 1855 as a newly discovered dogma; whereas it was as old as the world. The Virgin Mary is not a person, it is a metaphysical conception of the ancients, who did not believe in a special creation, or in a personal Christ.

The translators of the Bible have grossly imposed upon the world by concealing carefully every reference made in the Kabala concerning the female portion of the universal principle, and by rendering every feminine noun of the deity into a masculine one. It was a perversion of the teachings of the secret doctrine which cannot be too severely denounced. The pious men, who translated the Bible to suit their own interest, find their work condemned in the "Book of Concealed Mystery," chapter 1, verse 31, in which HVA and ALHIM are shown to be interchangeable, both being female types. Moreover, the "three mothers," the great female triad of the Kabala, is even before the triune father, and is held as one of the greatest secrets of the Kabalistic Arcanum. Thus the occultists agree with G. Massey, who places the great mother as first and above the father, and with the Pope's followers, who extol the Virgin Mary even above her son, recognizing her great power and the influence she exercises in the invisible world.

CHAPTER X.

5—6—8—9—12.

"As for wisdom, what she is, and how she came up, I will tell you and will not hide mysteries from you, but will seek her out from the beginning of her nativity, and bring the knowledge of her into light, and will not pass over the truth."—*Solomon.*

THE five-pointed star is also called the pentagram and the pentagon, in occult phraseology. It is supposed to represent the limbs of a man. This emblem is, like every other we have discussed in former chapters, of Egyptian origin. In the Ritual, and in the "Book of the Dead," the ceremonies for disposing of the defuncts are minutely described. While perusing those ancient manuscripts, one is vividly impressed with the Egyptians' grand conceptions of the mysteries of life and death. Their passage on this earth was only a daily preparation for the transformation that takes place when leaving. Thus the defunct man was portrayed as a pentagram, or five-pointed star, the points of which were supposed to represent the five limbs of a man, and he was also represented as a crocodile. Mr. Gerald Massey, the great symbologist, has identified the crocodile with the dragon of wisdom, as a type of intelligence. Now, in esotericism, the human soul, or mind, is the fifth principle; therefore the five-pointed star is the synthesis of the man of our present race. He is said to be developing the fifth principle.

In the Buddhist system of spiritual creative powers, reference is made to a group of so-called Dhyani-Buddhas, which is called the fifth group. It is linked mysteriously to the microcosmic pentagon, the five-pointed star typifying man. In India, as in Egypt, those celestial beings were identified with the crocodile, and said to have their abode in the zodiacal sign of Capricornius. The latter is still the crocodile in India nowadays. Whereas, the fifth principle, manas, or the human soul, is considered by occultists as the synthesis of the four lower principles. In the same manner the Greek philosophers made of ether, the fifth element, a combination of the other four. But the ether of the ancients was the akasa of the Hindus, and was entirely different from the element of the same name recognized and accepted by science. The latter is identical with the astral light, so graphically described by Eliphas Levi, and mentioned by St. Paul as the "Prince of the Air." It is one of the lower sub-divisions of primordial light.

In the myth of Priapus we find a dual being. There is a celestial Priapus, offspring of Bacchus and Venus, and a later Priapus, who has been identified with Agathodemon, the Gnostic saviour, and even with Abraxas. He is blended with the mythical record of the different races which have lived on this earth. He is represented as standing on the tree of life, and our own race is clearly indicated by the five branches which have been cut off. The holy of holies of the king's chamber in the great pyramid of Gizeh, the tabernacle of Moses, the holy of holies of the temple of Solomon, the ark of the covenant of St. Paul, Noah's ark, the lily in Gabriel's hand, the lotus of the Hindus, the ship of the Quichés, Jacob's pillar, the fiery serpents of the Hebrews, are identical symbols, related to number 5. "He" in Hebrew is 5, the glyph of the womb, and twice 5 is 10, or the phallic number expressed thus: ⊕ And again the double womb typifies the upper and lower heaven, or the spiritual and terrestrial duality; "as above, so below," says the Zohar.

All the ancient nations had a sanctum sanctorum, or adytum, in their temples, in which a sarcophagus, or tomb, was placed, from which the initiated candidate emerged in his impersonification of the resurrected solar god. The tomb was not only an emblem of spiritual re-birth, as expressed by St. Paul: "Knowing this, that our old man is crucified with him, that the body of sin might be destroyed, that henceforth we should not serve sin," but also of cosmic, solar, and human resurrection, or reawakening. Therefore the Jews, being exceedingly materialistic, set up their holy of holies as a sign of their monotheism, whilst it was but a universal phallic emblem rejected by the Kabalists, who recognized only Ain-Soph, and by the learned Sadducees, who respected nothing but the law.

St. Paul, in his Epistle to the Hebrews (chapter 9) says: "And, after the second veil, the tabernacle; which is called the holiest of all, which had the golden censer, and the ark of the covenant overlaid round about with gold, wherein was the golden pot that had manna, and Aaron's rod that budded, and the tables of the covenant; and over it the cherubims of glory shadowing the mercy-seat; of which we cannot now speak particularly." St. Paul did not wish to enter into the details as to the meaning of the ark, but he was not ignorant of symbolical lore. He knew well enough that the ark and the mount sprung from the same ideograph, for he declares forcibly the same tenet in the following passage addressed to the Hebrews: "Who serve unto the example and shadow of heavenly things, as Moses was admonished of God, when he was about to make the tabernacle; for see, saith he, that thou make all things according to the pattern showed to thee in the mount." The reader must bear in mind St. Paul's frequent admonitions that the "letter killeth." The mount, the tree, and the ark, are synonymous of the great mother, the womb of the universe. The "cherubims of glory" made the phallic glyph still more realistic. They were set up on the coffer, or ark of the covenant, facing each other, with their wings spread in such a manner as to present to the sight a perfect yoni. The same shaped yoni was worshiped by all ancient nations, the Hindus included. The latter have preserved the original pattern, which is to be seen to the present day in their temples, such as it was ages ago. St. Paul wished to divulge the secret only to those who understood the "spirit of the letter." No doubt can be entertained as to the meaning conveyed in the display of the Hebrew tabernacle, for it was further emphasized by the four mystic letters of the name Jehovah; the yod which, according to the Kabala, was the membrum virile, Hé, the womb, Vau ו, which is either a hook, crook or a nail, and Hé, which had another significance besides the womb; it was also an opening—in another word it was thus: Y(é) H (o) V (a) H, the male and female, or bi-sexual symbol. Michael's taunt is better understood when David's dance before the ark is revealed in its true light. As an illustration it is only one among many. The Old Testament does not solely contain allusions to customs that were as popular among the Jews as among the pagan nations of the world, but frequently denounces them in blunt terms. Out of the many examples we might cite we will quote but one. It is taken from the prophet Hosea: "They sacrifice upon the tops of the mountains, and burn incense upon the hills, under oaks and poplars and elms, because the shadow thereof is good; therefore your daughters shall commit whoredom, and your spouses shall commit adultery.

"I will not punish your daughters when they commit whoredom, nor your spouses when they commit adultery; for themselves are separated with whores, and they sacrifice with harlots; therefore the people that doth not understand shall fall."

The degrading ceremonies described by the prophet Hosea were one of the features of the "mount," "tree," "ark," "Tabernacle," or "great mother" worship, the remnants of which can be found nowadays in the Nautch-girls of the Hindu pagodas and the "Bad Woman" of Hong Kong. Such a deplorable state of affairs occurred, when the metaphysical conception of the "origin of all things" had dwindled down into the gross symbol of the Hebrew deity. Primitively, space was the boundless sidereal ocean, the waters upon which face the Spirit of God moved. Noah's ark typified the abstract idea of the "container" of all germs necessary to re-people the earth. The dove is the bird imaging the supremacy of spirit over matter, and the olive branch, the end of a cataclysm, a new period of life to be inaugurated on the earth. Therefore, we find the ark, or ship, in the Genesis of the Quichés in their description of the re-awakening of cosmos. It is reproduced in the mysteries as the navi-form Argha, as an ever-living emblem of the female generative power. It is the sacrificial chalice of the high priests of all the goddesses who typified the generative powers of nature; of Isis, Venus, Aphrodite, Astarte, and others. It has survived in the sacrifice of the mass among the Roman Catholics, the priest combining the dual emblem in the wine and water mixture which he drinks out of the mystic chalice.

When represented as standing on the globe, or on a crescent moon, the holy Virgin Mary is identical with Isis, Venus, Ursa Major, and the holy of holies of the Hebrews. Mary impersonates the ship of life, or nature, the abstract idea of the manifesting deity; and she is the navi, ark, or crescent under which the female symbol of universal idea is typified. The Virgin Mary, and the yoni of the Hindus, emerged from the same source, and the same idea is rendered by either of them. Therefore, the nave of the church must be traced back to the same origin, as it comes from navis-ship. It is the universal vessel of the Quichés, and of all archaic nations.

Hargrave Jennings says: "The ark contained a table of stone. That table was phallic, and identical with the same Jehovah—which, written in unpointed Hebrew with four letters, is Jeve, or J. H. V. H., the H being merely an aspirate and the same as E. This process leaves us the two letters I and V (in another form U); then if we place the I in the U we have the holy of holies, or the lingha and yoni." Why, are Christian missionaries blind or ignorant? Is there any difference between the holy of holies of the Jews and the lingha and yoni of the Hindus? We can see none whatever. Both are the result of an attempt at personifying an abstract ideal of the Infinite Spirit and nature. In Egypt and India the water-lily, or sacred lotus, was given the same interpretation, because it grows in the water, and is the bearer of its own seed. Hence the Archangel Gabriel appears to the Virgin Mary holding a lily in his hand.

Occultists consider the fifth sign of the zodiac as the center from which diverged the following three divisions. The latter were primitively contained in Leo, as their unity before Virgo-Scorpio split up, and became, by the interposition of Libra, three separate signs. Now, if we accept the inner interpretation of Leo as the Son or real Christ, we can easily perceive that Virgo, Libra, Scorpio are an astronomical myth related to the differentiation of matter. The seventh principle of the Buddhists is identical with the Christ of the Kabalists, and the elements which became manifested through Virgo, Libra, and Scorpio, were contained potentially in Leo. Virgo is the astral light, the virgin-mother of the world, the Illusion (Maya) of the Hindus. The arcane significance of Libra is easily fathomed when knowing that Scorpio typifies the "fall," as recorded in every cosmogony. The reconcentration of those three signs, and their re-absorption into Leo, will lead into the dissolution of the phenomenal world just in the same manner as their separation has brought it forth. Therefore, the ninth sign corresponds to the nine lights issuing from the crown (Zohar), and Aquarius being twice 5 represents not only the human body, the five limbs of man, but also the macrocosm, the outward veil of hidden deity, because both are external objects of perception.

Cassiopea, the chair or the throne, is composed of 5 stars disposed like an M. M is a sacred letter in occultism, because it combines the binary, *i. e.*, the male and female with their progeny, or the dual being above and the trinity below. It is equivalent to number 5, *i. e.*, a duad and a triad. It is also linked with Aquarius, thus ∿, the tenth sign of the zodiac, being frequently associated with the mythical crocodile, or aquatic monster. For the letter M stands for water, either in the Aryan or Semitic language. In occultism the pentagon is a sacred sign, and a divine monogram, expressing the initial letter of the most venerated names in the Pantheons of Pagan, Jewish or Christian nations. For example, the fifth Buddha is called Maitreya; Minerva is the goddess of wisdom; Mary is the mother of the Messiah; and Moses is drawn out of the water (Exodus) by Pharaoh's daughter. The Christian Christ is intimately related to water baptism, the fishes of the zodiac, and the water-lily.

In number 6 we must consider the hexagon, or six-pointed star, as the six limbs of the microprosopus. It is one of the symbols of the Christian Kabalists, who represented, under the figure of a double triangle, the six principles emanating from the light of the manifested Logos, or word. They called it the "lesser face," or countenance, and held it to be the prototype of man on the terrestrial plane. In Hinduism the same ideograph is symbolized by Fohat, or the seven sons, the two triangles being likewise synthesized by the point in the center. It answers to the bride, or our earth, of the Kabalists. Those two triangles are frequently designated under the name of Solomon's seal. They typify the union of the two sexes. The six-pointed star refers also to the six powers, or forces of nature, the six planes of consciousness, and the six principles of men, all of which emanate from the central point as seven, the perfect number. We must bear in mind that the heavenly virgin mother, known under different denominations, but still identical in every philosophical system, is the abstract principle, source of all differentiation, in the visible universe. Hence, the limbs of the microprosopus are ten and six respectively. The Kabala teaches that the "Fiat Lux" of the initial chapter of Genesis, is to be applied to the evolution of the Sephiroth, and not to light, the material substance which we know of. Rabbi Simeon expresses it explicitly in the following words: "O companions, companions, man as an emanation was both man and woman, Adam Kadmon, verily, and this is the sense of the words, 'Let there be light and it was light,' and this is the twofold man

(Zohar)." It becomes obvious that the "Fiat Lux" of Genesis does not refer to the Adam of our race, for in him the androgyne, or dual being, was separated. Therefore, figure 6, or the double is the mythical earth in its autumn and winter sleep waiting for Fohat, the bride, or the higher Sephiroth, to infuse life and spirit into it, at the reawakening period, or spring and summer.

The sage Richi had seven wives; six of them were bad; the hidden one was the only virtuous one. Number 6 is also linked with the Svastica, or Yaina-cross, and under this aspect is replete with meanings, because it embraces the whole space, namely, north, south, west, east, zenith and nadir. It is said that the initial letters of the name Jesus Christ are to be interpreted in numbers, and that their numerical value is 600. The same figure is to be applied to the sign A. O., the Alpha and Omega, the Beginning and End, being sixfold, as, north, south, east, west, height, and depth. The same idea is personified in the Hindu god Kârtikêya, who has six heads, and the Christ, or Horus, of the Gnostics, has six names, and partakes of a sixfold nature. There are three fires and three waters in occultism; the upper triangle with its apex upwards is masculine, and the lower triangle being reversed is feminine, thus typifying unity in both sexes, or rather the two sexes united. Such is the glyph embodied in the sixfold Christ, or the two triangles.

Number 6 is one of the fundamental figures of the mystic system, because it typifies the first emanation of the Logos, Word, or Christ, an emanation of the upper Sephirothal triad. The latter is essentially linked with the group called the "Lions of Fire," because they are related esoterically to the zodiacal sign of "Leo." They form the nucleus of the archetypal world.

In mystic reckoning 7 is an outgrowth of number 6; it gives rise to a combination which requires always one more which "is" and yet "is not." None has embodied this grand conception in his writings better than St. John in his masterpiece, "Revelation:" "I saw a woman sit upon a scarlet colored beast, full of names of blasphemy, having seven heads and ten horns. The seven heads are seven mountains on which the woman sitteth; and there are seven kings; five are fallen and one is, and the other is not yet come; and when he cometh, he must continue a short space."

And the beast that was and is not, is stamped forever in the starry heavens as the genitrix and her son, or the Great Bear and Lesser Bear. It is the foundation-stone of the mythos which began with the virgin-mother sitting upon the waters. Then underwent a change of symbolism, and was transformed into a solar glyph, when the Stellar deity ceased to be the time-keeper.

If we wish to search in the traditional records of

all the ancient nations, we will always discover similar features in their virgin mothers, and their numerical value will correspond to the figure 666, attributed by St. John to the beast of Revelation. Shushnah, the lily, is 666. The Hebrew Hesther is analogous to the Egyptian Shetar, or the betrothed, both answering to the description of the Kabalistic Bride, who is also the Beast. Isis, Venus, Minerva, the Virgin Mary, the Beast, etc., are symbolized either by the sistrum three S's or 666, and again the lotus lily. They are identical types, for they were evolved from the double constellation of the seven stars, hence, the beast was androgynous. But its mythical transformation was due to the cyclic changes that occurred in the course of time, when it became the six-headed dragon: "And I saw one of his heads as it were wounded to death; and his deadly wound was healed; and all the world wondered after the beast." Until now the beast had the "feet of a bear, according to the astronomical mythos, and the attributes of the Virgin Mother; but in its second aspect it is only six-headed, though its deadly wound was healed." And the woman who sat on the seven hills, which were seven kings, and also the seven-crowned heads of the beast, or Egyptian dragon, has never lost her prominent position. She is enthroned on the seven hills of the "Eternal City (Rome), where she divides with the second "beast" the divine honors proffered to her by the Popish clergy: "And I beheld another beast coming up out of the earth; and he had two horns like a lamb, and he spake like a dragon." It is evidently the sun entering the sign of the Ram, an emblem adored by the Christian world. This symbolism was continued from the Egyptians, who represented the second beast in its new phase of the "third beast, as a ram or lamb with its six heads on the crocodile, who is always identical with the dragon."

"It is not correct," says Madame Blavatsky, "to refer to Christ as some theosophists do, as the sixth principle in man, or, in Hindu phraseology, as Buddhi. The latter *per se* is a latent and passive principle, the spiritual vehicle of Atman, inseparable from the manifested universal soul. It is only in union, and in conjunction with self-consciousness, that Buddhi becomes the higher self and the divine, discriminating soul. Christos is the seventh principle, if anything."

"And the beast that was, and is not, even he is the eighth, and is of the seven, and goeth into perdition." Revelation, chapter 17. Here we have the primitive emblem of the genitrix, or the Ogdoad, as embodied by the Great Bear and her seven sons. It is a form of the boundless, of the infinite, reproduced *ad infinitum* by every nation, as the primary gods. In Akkad, or Assyria, they are neither males nor females, but among the Quichés they are half males, half females, for they impersonate the struggles between the rulers of the upper and lower realms. In its primordial aspect the beast is eight, then as the manifesting deity it becomes seven, the second beast. The latter by losing one head is 666, or the six-headed dragon, which "goeth into perdition," and re-appears transformed into the solar god, or Christos.

The Ogdoad is a symbol of the abyss, of the spiral motion of cycles, and is also related to the glyph of the Caduceus, Mercury's hieroglyph. Without him neither Isis nor Osiris could accomplish anything. He was represented with the Caduceus, the crescent, or the lotus, when typifying the philosophical Mercury, and with a reed or a roll of parchment, when personifying the adviser of Isis.

In reality, the Ogdoad is understood frequently as the dual four, which is identical with the below and above, the boundless infinite, from whom emanated the Logos, or Word. "The Word that in the beginning was with God, and that also was a God." The Christians apply it to Jesus Christ, but they must not forget that among the pagans, Mercury was the Word, the messenger of God.

Another typical symbol of the seven growing out of the eight primitive gods, we find represented in the mythical Melchizedek of the Hebrew scriptures, who is represented as the just one, because he is lord of the ecliptic, or balance. It is an astronomical allegory arising from the seven planets, or great gods, who were evolved from the eight primordial types. They appear in the traditions and records of ancient peoples, as the mighty ones, the divine instructors of mankind.

Hermes is portrayed sometimes armless, under the form of a cube, to express the power of speech and eloquence. It is he, as Mercury, who scatters through the Universe the seminal principle that fecundates nature. Mercury, Hermes, Jesus Christ, the Logos, the Word, are all abstract conceptions embodying the same eternal truth.

Number 9 is the triple ternary. Occultists consider it as an unlucky number; they claim it to be the antithesis of number 6. However, the Zohar introduces number 9 in the initial scene of cosmic evolution, as follows: "When he first assumed the form he caused nine splendid lights to emanate from it, which shining through it diffused a bright light in all directions; that is, his own with the nine together made ten or Ⓘ." The Zohar is one of the books containing the secret teachings of the Jewish initiates. The Word Zohar means light, and the passage just quoted answers entirely to the first chapter of St. John's Gospel, in which he says: "He was not the light, but was sent to bear witness of that light," for "by him all things were made."

In a work called the "Book of God," a picture describing Paradise according to Brahminical theology reproduces a seven-stepped mount, with a flat top, in the midst whereof a square table is spread. The latter is ornamented with nine precious stones and a silver bell, and upon the table lies a silver rose, which is the shrine of two women, who are only one in reality, but they are two in appearance. They are the dual beings, the celestial and terrestrial types underlying every ancient religious system of this world. "The lower world," says the Zohar, "is created after the pattern of the upper; and everything existing above is to be found, as it were, in a copy on the earth."

It was the highest deity itself which, according to Plato, built the universe in the geometrical form of the "Dodecahedron," and its "first begotten" was born of chaos and primordial light. The same ideograph was reproduced by the Quichés in a tree covered with ten fruits. By the tree stood a male and a female ready to pick the fruit from it, thus making up the twelve, or Dodecahedron of the Universe. The latter is symbolized in Western esotericism by the Sephirothal tree, or Adam Kadmon of the Kabalists; while Brahma represents the Pythagorean geometrical figures, that is, the Dodecahedron in the East.

In their primitive character the two first principles of "space and sky" were overshadowed by the "concealed breath" of Kneph. They evolved the tree with the ten fruits from which emanated the upper triad, or upper Sephiroth, and the seven lower Sephiroth. No nation undertook to unite the absolute Be-ness with cosmic evolution, except the Aztecs, who used to celebrate a festival called the arrival of the thirteen great gods; but it is rather an anomaly disavowed by the generations who received and preserved the early teachings of Archaic races. Twelve great orders of creative powers are linked in occultism with the twelve signs of the zodiac. But seven of those divine hierarchies are connected with the seven planets. From the twelve chief hierarchies which are recorded in the zodiac sprung the main points of theological legends. It would be preposterous to imagine that the twelve wonders performed by Hercules were only an astronomical allegory, referring to the twelve signs of the zodiac. It is only a small part of the truth, a deeper meaning underlies the myth so often debated by the Greeks, who were aware of its mystic significance. Even the Jews recognize the deep import attached to number twelve by adopting it in their political and religious fanes. The twelve tribes of Israel displayed on their respective banners the twelve signs of the zodiac, which were originally only hieroglyphs, before they were translated into pictures. Even in their temple of Jerusalem the four lunar subdivisions were surrounded by the twelve signs of the zodiac, and though we find therein the seven lights of the candlestick, we know that the high priest wore twelve precious stones, uniting the symbol of the seven planets, or planetary symbology, to the zodiacal myth. The "book of the Kings" places the zodiacal cult on par with the lunar and solar worship.

Christianity has not renounced the Jewish symbology, for the twelve wonders of Hercules are sculptured over the porticoes of several cathedrals, such as the Church of Cognac, the northern entrance to "Notre Dame" of Paris, the Cathedral of Strassburg, the Basilica of Saint Denis, etc. Even the papal chair, when cleaned in 1662, still had the twelve wonders of Hercules portrayed in true pagan fashion. Moreover, it is prescribed by the Roman Church that while consecrating churches, the walls should be signed with the chrisma, in the shape of a cross, twelve times in twelve different places. We may notice also the thirty-six crossings of the Syrian liturgy, which corresponded to the same number of the decans in the zodiac. The latter were thirty-six crossing-stars, wherefrom the Christian liturgy has been derived. In Revelation, St. John says: "In the midst of the street of it, and on either side of the river, was there the tree of life, which bare twelve manner of fruits, and yielded her fruit every month; and the leaves of the tree were for the healing of the nations." Chapter 22. We may here safely conclude that number 12 bore the same mystical significance among all the ancient civilized nations of our globe. It was the starting-point of every cosmogony which culminated into the phenomenal world, and was recorded in the twelve zodiacal signs. Hence the latter were first eight, then ten, and at last twelve, as they embodied successively the evolution of the manifesting principle on the material plane.

In the sublime description of the thirteen divisions of the Beard of Macroprosopus, which is frequently denominated the Crown, and also the Ancient One, occultists recognize the glyph for unity, because the Hebrew word Achad is synonymous with one—unity adds up for thirteen. Therefore the thirteen great gods of the Aztecs may have been derived from the same ideograph.

CHAPTER XI.

ANCIENT AND MODERN PHILOSOPHICAL SCHOOLS.

"The priests who officiated in these sacred solemnities, were called hierophants, or, revealers of holy things."—*Eleusinian Mysteries.*

AT the dawn of the Christian era, about the time signaled as marking the birth of Jesus Christ, the civilized world was divided into two camps, each one representing a different system of philosophical teachings. The Greeks and Romans were followers of a simple mode of thought and reasoning, and among them the word philosophy meant the pursuit and love of wisdom; while the votaries of Gnosticism were scattered all through Persia, Syria, Chaldea, Egypt, and even Palestine. By the word gnosis they understood the perfection and full attainment of wisdom itself, the tenets of their doctrine being all derived from a fundamental principle of unity, or deism. Hence, they professed themselves to be the restorers of the true knowledge of God, which they claimed was lost in the world. Both systems had leaders who have become celebrated. They gained numerous adherents at the start, but afterwards split, and subdivided into innumerable sects. For centuries, the Greek philosophers have survived in their writings. It will perhaps not be amiss to enumerate the most famous philosophical schools which flourished in Athens, as the seat of learning. There were the Epicureans, who taught that, wisely consulted, pleasure was the only attainable object of man's life on this earth; the Academics held doubt and skepticism as the height of wisdom; the Stoics maintained that indifference to all occurring events was true philosophy; the Aristotelians were named after their master, Aristotle. They conducted the most subtle debates on religion and social duties, declaring that, under a scientific point of view, the deity resembled the regulated motion of a machine, and was entirely regardless of human affairs. The Platonists were the disciples of the famous philosopher Plato. His teachings re-echoed the Egyptian doctrine in many respects. Through his friendly relations with the Egyptian hierophants, he had become imbued with their mode of thought concerning the immortality of the soul, the manifestation of a divine man who should be crucified, the rewards and punishments of a future life, and the transmigration of souls, known also as métempsychosis. And last, but not least, of all, appeared the Eclectics, who, as their name indicates, selected, out of all the different tenets of the above-enumerated schools, what they considered wise and reasonable, and founded a new and revised doctrine with its head establishment at Alexandria. A man called Potamon is credited with having been the ingenious teacher of the new doctrine, though his followers held the divine Plato in the highest esteem.

Thus, Alexandria was the seat of learning at the time assigned as the birth of Jesus Christ, and as corresponding to the era of Augustus, the great Roman emperor. It was in a flourishing condition, provided with the first and greatest library that ever was in the world, and a most famous university. Thither flocked the masters of all civilized nations, and from it were dealt out, as the craft needed, the most part of the holy legends, sacred mysteries, and inspired writings, which are presently in possession of the Christian world, though in a second-hand fashion. All the most valued manuscripts of the Christian Scriptures are known to be Codices Alexandrini. Foremost among them is the New Testament, which was originally written in Greek, because it was concocted by the monks of the great University of Alexandria. Eusebius, the greatest authority of the early Christian Church, confesses that the writings of the Eclectics, who were also the Therapeuts of Egypt, and the Essenes of Philo, were the same identical writings as our own Gospels. St. Paul denounces them in his Epistle to the Colossians in the following terms: "Beware lest any man spoil you through philosophy and vain deceit, after the tradition of men, after the rudiments of the world, and not after Christ." And again in the Epistle to Timothy, when he says, "But shun profane and vain babblings, for they will increase unto more ungodliness." This passage tends to show that he did not belong to any organized society—he was simply an itinerant therapeut, or healer. For, so far as his doctrine of Christ is concerned, it answers to the different Christ-types of the Western and Eastern philosophical schools. Even the monogram I H S, inserted in a circle of rays of glory, belonged to Bacchus for centuries before Jesus Christ inherited it from the pagan mysteries. The three Greek letters I H S are read like "yes," which is synonymous with the sun, of which Bacchus was one of the most reverenced personifications. By adding "us" it becomes Latinized as Jesus, or Yesus. The same circle of glory, expressive of the sun's rays of light, make the identity of the Christian Christ with Bacchus most complete.

It is, however, incontrovertible that the source of the doctrines contained in the New Testament is traceable to Gnosticism, or Eastern wisdom. Even the Old Testament is frequently termed the Chaldean Paraphrases, because the first translations of it date from the time following the Babylonian captivity. Now, the Gnosis contained the doctrines of the Magi, Persians, Chaldeans, Arabians, Egyptians, and even Hindus. That the Eastern philosophy was held in high esteem, even among the Jews, we cannot doubt; for does not St. Matthew say, "Behold, there came wise men from the East to Jerusalem." Was it not in India that the first allegory of Christ was gotten up? Was not Krishna the same identical personage as Jesus, and his virgin-mother given a similar name as Jesus' mother, Maia, the significance thereof being identical with the Christian word Mary?

Such a digression would be futile, if the attempt to revive the ancient teachings had not met with considerable success nowadays. The ancient therapeutists, or healers of soul and body, have been resurrected in the Christian scientists. The Gnostics, Rosicrucians, and Neo-Platonists, have always managed to keep a semblance of life to the present day, while the great bulk of esoteric knowledge has continued in a flourishing condition in the land of wonders, which is India. In the latter years a flood of information has been poured upon the world by a society denominated the "Theosophical," the leaders thereof claiming connection with initiates of Eastern occult wisdom. Their aim is to form the nucleus of a universal brotherhood of man without distinction of race, color, sex, or creed. They wish to promote the study of Aryan and other Eastern literatures, religions, and sciences, and offer an opportunity to students of the occult side of nature, to investigate unexplained laws, and the psychical powers inherent in the human race. Their teachings have no special features of either the Chaldean, Jewish, or Egyptian system, but are rather inclined towards the Buddhistic doctrine. In the precedent chapters frequent references have been made to the esotericism of every prominent nation. Our work would be incomplete in the present stage of researches in the field of occultism, if the theory of re-incarnation and the law of Karma were left out.

Re-incarnation and the law of Karma go hand in hand, one is the cause and the other the result, *i. e.*, if no Karma was generated there would be no re-incarnation; such is the theosophical theory and it is nothing more or less than an old idea clothed in a new garb. The Egypto-Christian doctrines of original sin, and of the necessity of being born again, are misconceptions of the text of the New Testament, of the Pythagorean metempsychosis, and of the trials of neophytes prior to, their initiation into the mysteries.

Pythagoras was born at Samos (Greece), in the year 586 B. C. He was a teacher of the purest system of morals ever propounded to man. He is the famous discoverer of the celebrated theorem of the first book of Euclid, and to him is attributed our theory of the planetary system. He is also characteristically associated with the doctrine of metempsychosis, which was inculcated into him by the Egyptian priests, whose distinguished pupil he was. After having admitted the immortality of our souls, or "nous," as the Greeks termed it, it was but a subsequent step to inquire what became of them. Hence, the institution of those mysteries so sublimely treated of by ancient writers, and especially by Virgil in his Æneid, and by the Egyptians in their manuscripts and sculptured stones.

The time that elapsed from one re-incarnation to another varied from one thousand years in Pythagorean reckonings to three thousand, according to the Egyptian traditions. Greeks and Egyptians agreed on the main points, however; they believed that after drinking of the waters of Lethe, which caused a forgetfulness of all past events, the soul, under the leadership of Mercury, the Logos, or Word of God, was born of water and wind, synonymous with Puff or Holy Ghost, and launched again into humanity. It was openly taught that the souls of men who had been wicked during their former existence, were born in sin; hence, the original sin of Christian theology, and the calamitous circumstances that surrounded the evil-doers until they had worked off all the bad influences which they had brought upon themselves. If Christians were not blind to the truth, they would find the Pythagorean theories as concerning the punishment of crime, repeatedly illustrated in the New Testament. The reader must bear in mind that the identity of the historical Jesus has naught to do with the fact that the gospels uphold the doctrine of re-incarnation. In sober truth, the rebuke of Jesus to Nicodemus, the ruler of the Jews, is the most striking recognition of the same tenet. "Art thou a master of Israel, and knowest not these things," is the most convincing proof that there was no excuse at the time for an educated person not to be conversant with the subject.

The best illustration, however, is to be found in St. John, chapter 11: "And as Jesus passed by, he saw a man which was blind from his birth. And his disciples asked him, saying, Master, who did sin, this man or his parents, that he was born blind?" This question corroborates our opinion that the Jews were adherents to the Egyptian theories of re-incarnation, otherwise how could we account for the severe invective which they launched against the blind man: "Thou wast altogether born in sins, and dost thou teach us? And they cast him out." Neither does Jesus discountenance the same ideas, when expressed by his disciples: "Some say that thou art John the Baptist, some Elias, and others Jeremias, or one of the prophets." Not only does the New Testament inculcate the Pythagorean conception of metempsychosis, but the Old Testament is replete with striking illustrations of the same principle. Now, that the theosophical teachers have revived the ancient religious systems, they advocate, as we have stated before, the theory of re-incarnation, which is most distasteful to great many Christians, because they read their Bible without understanding it. In other words, they have not yet eaten the "book" of Revelation. Mr. Sinnett, in his esoteric Buddhism, created quite a sensation on account of his startling statements on many perplexing points.

He gave definite and absolute figures, fixing the number of times that a soul should be re-incarnated, and the number of years that should elapse from one re-incarnation to another. Before the publication of "Esoteric Buddhism," Madame Blavatsky had declared, in "Isis Unveiled" that no re-imbodiment took place except in the case of premature or accidental deaths, including defective organizations, such as born idiots. Now, in her last work, the "Secret Doctrine," which is a corollary of "Isis Unveiled," she expounds her opinion as follows: " The cycle of metempsychosis for the human monad is closed, for we are in the fourth round of the fifth root race. The reader will have to bear in mind at any rate one who has made himself acquainted with 'Esoteric Buddhism,' that the stanzas which follow in this book and book 2, speak of the evolution in our fourth round only. The latter is the cycle of the turning-point, after which, matter having reached its lowest depths, begin to strive onward and to get spiritualized with every new race, and with every fresh cycle. Therefore, the student must take care not to see contradiction where there is none, as in 'Esoteric Buddhism' rounds are spoken of in general, while here, only the fourth, or our present, round is meant. Then it was the work of formation, now it is that of reformation and evolutionary perfection."

The late president of the Hermetist Society of London, Dr. Anna Kingsford, expresses herself thus: "Re-incarnation pertains only to the true soul. The astral soul, or earthy envelope, does not again become incarnated; so that they are not in error who assert that a person is never twice incarnate. That which transmigrates is the essential germ of the individual, the seat of all his divine potencies. In some this exists as a mere dim spark, and in others, as a luminous sun." Besides the Hermetists, the late Dr. Anna Kingsford has many admirers among students of mysticism; for the "Perfect way, or the finding of Christ," has won her a distinguished position as an expounder of the philosophy of the thrice great Hermes. Therefore, her opinion acquires considerable weight, backed, as it is, by the erudition of her co-worker, Mr. Edward Maitland.

Among the theosophists, Franz Hartman enjoys a well-deserved reputation as a favorite author on occult subjects. In his "Magic White and Black," he has very ingeniously defined what theosophists mean by re-incarnation, as we can perceive by perusing the subsequent sentences: "If, as it frequently happens, children show the same or similar talents and intellectual capacities as their parents, such a fact is by no means a proof that the parents of the child's physical body are also the parents, or producers, of its intellectual germ; but it may be taken as an additional evidence of the truth of the doctrine of re-incarnation, because the spiritual monad of the child would be naturally attracted, in its efforts to re-incarnate, to the bodies of parents, whose mental and intellectual constitution would correspond nearest to its own talents and inclinations, developed during a previous earthly life. Characters may exist independent of external conditions; the latter can only modify, but not create, the former. The best soil will not produce an oak tree unless an acorn is present, and a cholera bacillus will not produce cholera where the 'predisposition' to that disease does not already exist. Forms may facilitate the development of character, but they do not create it, and persons that appear in every respect alike may be of a very different character.

"How can we account for such moral and intellectual discrepancies in forms that are nearly alike, as long as we shut our eyes to the truth that that which is essential in a being, whether rational or irrational, is its character, and that its form is only the external expression of that internal and invisible character, which may survive after the form has ceased to exist, and after the dissolution of the form finds its expression again in another form. Forms die, but their character remains unchanged after their death, preserved in the Astral Light, like the thoughts of man stored up in his memory, after the events that called them into existence have passed away. A character does neither die nor change after it has left the form, but, after a time of rest in the subjective state, it will re-imbody itself again in a new-born objective form, to grow and change its nature during the life of form. Seen from this standpoint, 'death is life,' because, during the time that death lasts, that which is essential in a form does not change; life is death, because only during life in the form the character is changed, and old tendencies and inclinations die and are replaced by others.

"Our passions and vices may die while we live; if they survive us they will be born again. Each seed will grow best in the soil that is best adapted to its constitution; each human monad existing in the subjective state will be attracted at the time of its incarnation to parents, whose qualities may furnish the best soil for its own tendencies and inclinations, and whose moral and mental attributes may correspond to its own. The physical parents cannot be the progenitors of the spiritual germ of the child; that germ is the product of a previous spiritual evolution, through which it has passed in connection with former objective lives. In the present existence of a being, the character of the being that will be its successor, is prepared.

"Therefore, every man may be truly said to be his own father; for he is the incarnated result of the personality which he evolved in his last life upon the planet, and the next personality which he will represent in his next visit upon this globe, is evolved by him during his present life." This passage, drawn from a work indorsed by the high priestess of theosophy, Madame Blavatsky, affords us a thorough insight into the views held by the leaders of the present theosophical propaganda. We leave to our readers the task of scrutinizing the rules set down by Franz Hartman. We may apply to his theories on re-incarnation the benefit of the lesson involved in the following anecdote: A French teacher was remonstrating with a bright pupil of hers because the latter was exceedingly careless in spelling the word "quelque." "I will," said Madame, "explain over again the rule which applies to that word, and I wish to impress it on your mind in such a manner that you will not forget it."

"Never mind the rule, Madame, I pray you to begin with the exceptions," exclaimed the irrepressible American pupil.

Thus, we might also consider the exceptions in the matter of the above quotation, without incurring the reproach of slighting its merits. The greatest objection that can be raised is not only that in a family of ten children, born from the same parents, under the same circumstances, surrounded by the same elements, each one will eventually develop different tendencies; but, moreover, it is a frequent occurrence to hear the incidental remark of a good man having raised a corrupted and villainous son, and it is noteworthy that many men who were the leading personages on this world's theatrical stage, having at their disposal the resources of powerful nations, have been unable to bequeath their genius to their children. We will close this argument with Madame Blavatsky's description of the use and power of the third eye, or Cyclopean eye. She says: "The eye of Siva did not become entirely atrophied before the close of the fourth race. When spirituality and all the divine powers and attributes of the devaman of the third had been made the hand-maidens of the newly-awakened physiological and psychic passions of the physical man, instead of the reverse, the eye lost its powers. But such was the law of evolution, and it was, in strict accuracy, no fall. The sin was not in using those newly-developed powers, but in misusing them; in making of the tabernacle, designed to contain a god, the fane of every spiritual iniquity. And if we say 'sin,' it is merely that everyone should understand our meaning, as the term Karma would be the right one to use in this case; while the reader who would feel perplexed at the use of the term spiritual instead of physical iniquity, is reminded of the fact that there can be no physical iniquity. The body is simply the irresponsible organ, the tool of the psychic if not of the 'spiritual man.' While in the case of the Atlanteans, it was precisely the spiritual being which sinned, the spirit element being still the 'master' principle in man, in those days. Thus, it is in those days that the heaviest Karma of the fifth race was generated by our monads. Therefore the fresh pouring in, or arrival, of new monads had ceased as soon as humanity had reached its full physical development. No fresh monads have incarnated since the middle point of the Atlanteans. Hence, remembering that save in the case of young children and of individuals whose lives were cut off by some accident, no spiritual entity can re-incarnate, such gaps alone must show that the number of monads is necessarily finite and limited. Moreover, a reasonable time must be given to other animals for their evolutionary progress."

Hence, the assertion that many of us are now working off the effects of the evil Karmic causes produced by us in Atlantean bodies. "The law of Karma is inextricably interwoven with that of re-incarnation." From the above quotations, it becomes obvious that the theosophical leaders do not entertain such wild ideas about re incarnation as have been advanced by partisans of Allan Kardec, and others belonging to the same school. We repeat our assertions, that our baptism had no other foundation except to inculcate the necessity of being re-born, to become regenerated. The idea culminated in the institution of the mysteries, and degenerated into the Christian baptism, which is a mock ceremony of the pagan fanes. · The immoral effect of the doctrine of atonement for sin, is the principal cause of crimes. "When thou thyself art guilty, why should a victim die for thee?" exclaims scornfully the poet Ovid. The perverse tendencies of such teachings are noted daily by philosophers and philanthropists. "Were a wise man," remarks Bishop Kidder, "to choose his religion by the lives of those who profess it, perhaps Christianity would be the last religion he would choose." Let us judge the tree by its fruit; if Christianity has produced no moral effects in the world, where is its merit?

The inflexible law of Karma is far more conducive to good results, for no matter how deep the offense, the eternal law of progress is like the light shining in the dark, to the ignorant one who is wicked because he is ignorant. Karma is identical with the Christian Providence and the pagan Prometheus. "He who sees beforehand," was emblematically portrayed as an eye surrounded with rays of glory, as though he was casting his beams of light upon our poor suffering humanity. The Christians have adopted the same type to represent their divine providence, who is nothing else but Karma. The law that regulates the course of globes and men cannot be propitiated; it is as inflexible as the "Fates;" the word in Greek expresses it graphically, "Be it so."

Still Prometheus is also the sun-Christ, not lacking even the fisherman, Oceanus, who is also Peter; because Petreus is a synonym of Oceanus, and the Christ is also portrayed with the fish, which word has been adopted as the initials of the cross, though the original inscription could not have been but Hebraic, if such ever existed. We have explained the myth of the Christ and the cross, therefore we will return to our subject.

Occultists claim that no form can be given to anything which does not exist already on the subjective plane. Therefore a man cannot conceive an idea, even as an effort of his own imagination, without its having a prototype, spiritually speaking. Hence, material man is simply an evolution of his own self, and must have existed prior to his appearance on this earth. Karma, or the effects he has generated in former lives, constitutes the germ, or essence, of his own life, and regulates the events of it. Consequently, it is reasonable to suppose that our planetary system being so intimately linked together, celestial bodies should to a certain point determine the good or bad luck of each individual. We cannot deny that there is an occult side of nature, of which we feel the effects in an unaccountable, yet unmistakable manner. The elements, which enter into the composition of our body, are the causes which bring forth the events of our earthly life, because the affinity existing between men, and the elementals corresponding to fire, air, water, and ether, establishes a connection between them. The element which predominates in a certain condition becomes the ruling element through life, though the body can undergo transformation through re-birth, as St. Paul has expressed it so explicitly: "Knowing this, that our old man is crucified with him [Christ], that the body of sin might be destroyed, that henceforth we should not serve sin." This is the re-birth, which was acquired by the candidate who became initiated into the holy mysteries of regeneration. St. Paul expresses still more forcibly the idea he wished to convey to his followers, in his Epistle to the Colossians: "In whom also ye are circumscribed with the circumcision made without hands, in putting off the body of the sins of the flesh by the circumcision of Christ. Buried with him in baptism, wherein also ye are risen with him through the faith of the operation of God, who hath raised him from the dead. And you being dead in your sins and the uncircumcision of your flesh, hath he quickened together with him, having forgiven you all trespasses."

If Christians were not absolutely blind to the truth they would perceive that St. Paul entertained just exactly the same notions about dead-letter ceremonies as the ancient philosophers and teachers. The forgiveness referred to in the above quotation is not a popish absolution, nor Christ, the personal or historical Jesus, paying for the crimes of mankind. For he remarks pointedly: "Let no man therefore judge you in meat or in drink, or in respect of a holy day or of the new moon, or of the Sabbath-days; which are a shadow of things to come, but the body is of Christ." Therefore, he condemns the dead-letter system thought to be fit only for the rabble; the same system now in vogue, especially among the Romish devotees, poor deluded victims of reverend rogues, who keep them in ignorance, which is equivalent to wickedness on both sides.

We are reaping now the bad Karma created by the enlightened men of past ages, who, being afraid of popular prejudices, propagated a doctrine with two meanings, that is, a secret and a public one. The key to the inner interpretation having become, I will not say lost but *mislaid*, the real facts have dwindled down into ridiculous mummeries, and perverse translations of primitive conceptions. A time came when, after the introduction of Christianity, outspoken truth was dangerous; therefore wise men hid their sayings under the veil of symbolism. It has become now a sacred duty to poor misguided humanity, to reveal to men the naked meaning of the religious symbols and writings which have been manipulated with such great profit by their oppressors. "Knowledge is power," not in its worldly sense, but as expressed by the great French adept, Eliphas Levi. When the masses will become searchers after the truth, they will "believe because they will know," and in this alone resides real power.

Men alone are responsible for their actions, and no third party, no Saviour, can avert from them the consequences of their sins. "There is no judge over the wicked," says the Kabala, "but they themselves convert the measure of mercy into a measure of judgment." But it is in the 34th chapter of Exodus that we find the so-called Karmic law best expounded:, "And the Lord passed by before him, and proclaimed, The Lord, the Lord God, merciful and gracious, long-suffering, and abundant in goodness and truth; keeping mercy for thousands, forgiving iniquity, and transgression, and sin, and that will by no means clear the guilty; visiting the iniquity of the fathers upon the children, and upon the children's children, unto the third and to the fourth generation." This passage contains the key to the mysterious doctrine of reincarnation; it handles the knotty question with a masterly hand, and settles all debates on the subject.

Here we will conclude our researches in the realm of occult and natural symbolism. We entertained, at the start, an ardent desire to enlighten others who had dedicated less time than ourselves to such a deep subject. We feel confident that our attempt, though very imperfect, will aid those who wish to become conversant with the Kabala and other secret writings. The tendency of this work being to diffuse light on important religious matters, we have consulted competent authorities, and have tried to present their ideas to our readers in a lucid and clear manner. May we have attained our aim!

www.ingramcontent.com/pod-product-compliance
Lightning Source LLC
Chambersburg PA
CBHW020908230426
43666CB00008B/1367